Lübeck: A Wonderful Moment in Time

Secret soldier-spying, and other lessons of life, in a beautiful fairy tale city on the East/West German border.

by Don E. Johnson

Lübeck:
A Wonderful
Moment in Time

ISBN 0-615-12652-9

On the surface, *Lübeck: A Wonderful Moment in Time* may seem like just another army memoir, but it is actually about dealing with life, love and the pursuit of happiness in a strange and foreign land – post war West Germany. The nasty edginess of the cold war was still in full bloom, and so were a multitude of eager young *fräuleinin* seeking their way to the promised land, the United States. It started out being a history of my truly unique Army Security Agency detachment, the Lübeckers, but I found out shortly that I wasn't well versed enough to report its short and tumultuous history – plus a semi-official reportage had already been done. All I know for sure is what happened to me. Well, at least reasonably sure. And that is what this book is all about - plus anecdotes and tales from other Lübeckers who were more frisky and fearless than I was.

Thankfully.

Lübeck: A Wonderful Moment in Time **is dedicated to all Lübeckers, no matter the race, color, creed, nationality, sex era, or MOS.**

Acknowledgments

I wish to thank my wife, Norma, for putting up with me during the long months writing this book. Also for her insights, suggestions, critical evaluations, and eagle eye as an editor and grammar expert. (Decades spent as a "Language Arts" teacher.) Thanks also to others who allowed me to use their own written memoirs and notes; in particular, Dave Savignac who penned the more-or-less official history of the Lübeck detachment in "The Lübeckers - The U.S. Army Security Agency in Lübeck, West Germany 1954-1965;" Jack Weber's narrative, "Corporals We! Der Fuhrer and Me! (1957 - 1960 the Cold War);" Myron Havis, for his accounts of his Lübeck experience; Mort Weston, for his remembrances, such as they were, and all the other assorted nuts, screwballs, culture freaks and all-around good guys that bothered to publicly air some of their earlier "moments."

Most of the photographs, except a few, were taken by me or of me with my trusty Kodak Retina IIc. Many of them were originally color slides but had to be converted to black/white for this book.

Please excuse the few blurry ones as I was a rookie at photography way back then. Thanks to Bill McMaster for his postcard of the interior of the Riverboat, Richard Strader for his photos of Trafalgar Square, interior J-Haus, C-Strasse, and of himself with Marcus Kehrli. Thanks also to Dave Wrench for his aerial photo of the Blankensee site and Duain Shaw, Mike Raphael, and Harry Walthall for a few random shots.

The cover photo is mine; the Lübeck Holstentor in 2001.

What you are about to read is based mainly on my recollections, and since I have been known to forget a thing or two now and then, I apologize for any incorrect names, omitting anyone or anything else I may have mis-remembered.

It is what it was.

Foreword

My life as a Lübecker began at nearly the midpoint of what was a special time, in a special place, that existed for approximately 11 years, from 1954 to 1965. It is quite likely that this was a totally unique experience, with unique individuals doing unique things, that had never before existed in the U.S. Army, and unfortunately, or maybe, fortunately, never existed again. There were, over the years, only about 200 to 300 good men (and a few slackers) involved.

How special was it? In answer to that age-old question, "what did you do in the Cold War, Grandpa?" "Well, child, I was a specially trained agent that gathered information about the Russian armies and the Polish guards deep within the enemy territory of East Germany.

Sort of.

Let me tell you, it *was* something special. Our little detachment of specialists was the only group of Americans for miles around. We operated out of Lübeck, which is this sort of fairy-tale city that happened to be right smack-dab on the border between East and West Germany. This was very convenient for our kind of outfit.

We kept out mouths shut – heck , most of the people of Lübeck didn't even know we were there. Way back then our work was highly, highly classified. But no more, so it's ok to get into all this. To be honest, we figured out a way to do all this sneaky stuff without sacrificing life and limb.

Well, maybe just a little."

Yes, definitely, we were supposed to be a secret operation. However, according to Christa-Maria Hahn, *"**On the way into Berlin, the East German border guards knew I was engaged to Bill, even knew his serial number, and proceeded to tell me what he was doing**. I had no clue until then. It was scary to sit there and to be interrogated, but they must have felt I really knew nothing and let me go. They told me Bill was on "abhör Geräten" (listening devices). But I did not know that he spoke Russian until we were married."*

I salute you!

Lübeck: A Wonderful Moment in Time

CHAPTER 1: The Dream

I have dreamt cartoons, but more often than not, I dream complete movies or TV programs with a beginning, middle, and end. If I could remember half of them, I probably would be rich. I have dreamt in foreign languages, including one dream in French and one in Italian, although I don't speak more than two words in either language. One Italian dream that I'll never forget concerned one of Italy's greatest Renaissance architects, Filippo Brunelleschi. In it, a huge cathedral was under construction and I was watching. A horseman rode up and asked one of the laborers, *"Dove Brunelleschi?"* (Where's Brunelleschi?) He pointed toward a man sitting on a huge dappled horse and it was me! Wow! So nothing I dream surprises me anymore.

Except for one in particular. It seemed so real, but that's what lucid dreams do. Now though, it's pretty fuzzy and all I remember is a big room – like a dance hall - and I was trying to arrange tables, and people were milling around in slow-motion confusion. Like a TV set gone bad, some faces from long ago were fading in and out, and I realized these were faces I haven't seen for over 40 years. My God! My synapses were finally snapping together. There's Ade; there's Roach; there's La Jeunesse. There's Nellie and Mort. There's Renate, Annegret, and Sissi. There's Christiana and Carole. Whoa! Carole, what are you doing here? The faces were mostly from Lübeck. Lübeck, the beautiful city almost on the Baltic in far northern Germany. And here I was, dreaming away and apparently trying to organize a reunion. I vaguely recall standing in the midst of all this turmoil and arguing with somebody over which city would be most convenient for the most people. To be honest, it was a mess. Then I woke up.

When the morning fog finally cleared from my brain, and I realized I was actually awake, I knew this reunion thing was something I had to do. But how? I knew absolutely nothing about planning a reunion – of any sort. Not to mention one so important that I dreamt about it. So, still in my jockeys, I dashed to the computer and cranked up the internet. The search engine

Google pointed me to "army reunions," and 12 pages in I came upon the heading, "ASA LIVES!" and even stranger than any of my lucid dreams, here was a web site dedicated to my old outfit, the Army Security Agency, the watchdog of the Pentagon, the eyes, ears, nose and throat of the Army, the purveyor of all that's good and bad about the world we live in.

Further clicking led to a site named, "The Lübeck Association," something I couldn't even imagine existed. This was the whole deal; guest book, biographies, links, missing Lübeckers list, reunions. Reunions! Oh God, they've been having reunions for years and no one told me about them. Worse, last year, they had a big shindig in Lübeck itself, with the *Bürgermeister* there and all sorts of local dignitaries and former whores and no one told me about that either. Worst of all, my name, wasn't even on the missing Lübeckers list. No doubt, it was time to get un-missing.

I logged on, registered, and began reading through the notes in the guest book. What was there about Lübeck that was so special? Did we actually form a bond of some sort? It certainly looked like it. Did I begin to grow up there? Well, hopefully. And yet, after 40 years, my memory is still crystal clear.

Maybe not exactly clear as crystal, but not foggy, either. As I begin to look back, I realize how much I didn't know about our little secretive operation in Lübeck - it was supposed to be secret, not secretive, but didn't quite make it. As a 20 year old enlisted RA (Regular Army) schnook from Smalltownsville, Iowa, I had a job. I did it although I didn't have the foggiest notion of who, what, when and why. I did know where. But now, looking at a map of northern Germany, and finally combining some little known facts laying dormant in my fallow brain, it's apparent our mission in Lübeck was to keep our ears open for potential rumbling from the 74th Tank Guards or any other nasties, such as the 94th Motorized Guards, and others groups that were ensconced in and around *Schwerin*, just a few miles across the East German border and an occasional voice transmission from potential Polish speaking adversaries somewhere in the vicinity. In other words, if radio traffic from the Red Guards picked up substantially and ominously during non-maneuver times, our little 27 man outpost of cryptologists, (rhymes with proctologists

– with similar results) traffic analysts, Morse code interceptors, direction finders, Russian and Polish linguists and such would alert the world, jump into civilian clothes and get the hell out of Dodge, to return later when the nuclear ashes had settled, if we were lucky.

The ASA was the Army's contribution to the NSA, which is the big overseer in the sky. The smartest, brightest, and clean enough to pass a security clearance were plucked from the enlistees and aimed towards the Agency. I got in because, through friends who had served in the Air Force version, I was one of the few who knew that the ASA even existed, and had the foresight to enlist directly into it. However, since I missed only one question on the army entrance exam, (stupid me, I knew the answer.) I would have been asked anyway. I knew I was relatively intelligent, but some of the guys I hung out with put me definitely in the back row. Way in the back.

Each branch of the service had its version of the ASA, and all were given the same mission: to listen in to what the other side was doing and report it to people who could do something about it. The other side could be anyone, of course. Friend or foe. Despite my Iowa naiveté, I knew that spying is a serious and sometime deadly business, even if done from a radio console. Yes, it can be deadly. For example: the Israelis killed 34 and wounded 171 of our brothers in the Navy during their version of Pearl Harbor against the virtually unarmed spook ship USS Liberty in international waters off the coast of Israel in 1967. Too many ASA'ers were also casualties during the Vietnam police action.

Due to a serious "need to know" factor but more likely to the "I don't much care to know" factor, after perusing many web sites dedicated to the ASA, I find that it actually has a proud history of serving its nation well. In Korea, Vietnam, and virtually everywhere around the globe, it spread its electronic tentacles. Luckily for some, and me in particular, the tentacles put a bunch of us fortunate ASA'ers smack in the middle of the fairy tale city of Lübeck. I think a part of us will always remain there and I want to go back.

So I will.

CHAPTER 2: The Ride to Camelot

"I've learned that I found Camelot when I was 19 years old, and have been trying to regain it ever since." Dave "Tab" Black

It was cold. I was already freezing my butt off, and we hadn't even started. It was a late winter morning, frosty and clear, which was unusual for this part of Germany. I tossed my 60 pounds of duffel and a beat-up worthless carbine I had never fired, into the back of a two and a half ton U.S. Army truck with a big white star on each door and one on the hood. I boosted my Army Security Agency ass up and over the tailgate and a few other guys I didn't know followed. We were now cargo along with a pile of duffel bags, some odd boxes and a few smelly, semi-moldy woolen blankets.

We solemnly snuggled into the blankets; the big adventure was starting and we were ready. The driver came around, checked the tailgate, closed the canvas flaps, hopped back into his nice warm cab and we were off.

I knew the ride from Rothwesten, just outside Kassel, to Lübeck, in far northeastern West Germany was about 225 miles long. I calculated that it would be five or six hours of traveling time at the most. However, in the bitter cold, with internal organs slowly beginning to freeze up, it seemed as though we were traveling at a top speed of roughly seven and a half miles per hour. We stopped somewhere to thaw out, empty the icy yellow slush from our bladders and get a bite to eat, but that's all unclear. Maybe I was delirious or semi-conscious from the cold and bouncing around. Either way, deep down inside I was happy and more than a little bit apprehensive as we roared merrily up and down the hills and valleys of Hitler's nifty *Reichsautobahn*. To exactly what, I didn't know, but this was supposed to be to the Valhalla of all ASA personnel, to the Mission Possible, to Camelot, to ... what the hell - to Lübeck!

1. On the road to Lübeck

Not everybody was so lucky. In my case, I had apparently done something right, for out of the blue, I was suddenly assigned to the biggest cherry that any one of us could imagine. I was a MOS 058 radio intercept operator that worked in a big room filled with about a dozen other morse-code takers, bundles of wires and high-powered short-wave radio consoles. All this was in a nice newly converted Luftwaffe building in the middle of an antenna field in an Army Security Agency base near the tiny village of Rothwesten, in north central West Germany. I didn't ask why I was chosen, I just packed my bags and got ready. Since the Army placed such a high emphasis on winning medals, trophies, and the like, all I could think of was that this was Sergeant's what his name's way of repaying me. I had always been an athlete in high school, and since the age of 15 played about every position on a pretty good men's softball team in our itty-bitty town in Iowa. But being from such a tiny hamlet I didn't have much to show for it.

The past few months I had proven my worth as a standout Army athlete, playing and sometimes starring on the company softball, volleyball and basketball teams. The basketball team was my greatest glory as we tied for first in the league and I was voted co-mvp with a 29 point average - and that was playing against former college players. I even threw the javelin in a track meet in Heidelberg where I came in second with a magnificent Olympic non-qualifying heave of approximately 67 feet. (To be honest, there were only three of us entered in this particular competition and the winner, who showed both of us unenlightened ones how to do it, was a former college javelin hurler. He tossed it with ease about 250 feet, give or take a bit.) To me, it was just a neat way of getting time off from a boring job; to the company commander, wins and trophies equaled promotions, status and bragging rights.

A lot of good that did me, though as my butt got sorer and sorer and the rest of me got colder and colder. The day was thinking about turning dark and the jouncing around became more forceful and jittery as we were now riding on cobblestone or brick streets. I wondered if we had finally reached a city. We were too cold and numb and bored to care and, as it was impossible to see out except through a little narrow opening in the canvas back flap, no one even bothered to peek out. A few more miles of constant jittery-jouncing, a few sharp turns, and the big truck pulled into a street, pounded over one last rut and squeaked to a stop. I peeked out the back flap and immediately thought something was screwy as I could see that we had come to rest on a residential street. A short chubby-cheeked private, with Bohan stenciled on his name tag, walked behind the truck and shouted a welcome. Everybody out. Welcome to Lübeck! Just in time for supper. He untied the flap and let the tailgate drop with a loud thang. It was strangely noticeable that he did not say "chow." We reluctantly left our smelly blankets and slid gingerly out the back. There, before our semi-frozen eyes was a genuine house - almost a villa - and I slowly walked toward it to get a better look.

To me, a hick from the Iowa sticks, the house was amazing and I'll never forget my first impressions. It was three stories tall, narrow, grayish, outlined in big rectangular blocks and had a pointy Mansard-like roof line that emphasized its height. The third floor had a smallish bell-shaped façade centered by a pair of rectangular windows. It was all perfectly symmetrical.

Four steps led to the double front doors which each had a small oval-shaped window and were topped by a semi-circled arch and flanked by not two, but four dark gray rounded pillars. Looking closer, I could see that two pillars were completely round and two were half-pillars, so that would technically make only three. The rooms on both sides of the entrance also had nicely arched windows. Someone had already turned the lights on inside. The entrance porch was crowned with an iron-railed balcony that had glass French doors that must have led into someone's bedroom. The yard was outlined with an iron picket fence, I noticed, with sharp, pointed spear-like tops. Four square posts about four feet tall flanked the gate and in front of it all, a collection of jeeps and cars were parked on a wide tree-lined apron. I had never been this close to a house of such stature. I had seen large houses, of course, especially in magazines, but this was the first time I would be going inside one. Wow! This was complete! Balconies, pillars, arched doors and windows; iron pointed picket fences with a gate. I almost shouted, "Mom, I'm home!"

This was *Jürgen-Wullenwever Strasse* #10, also known as JW 10 and dubbed later by the uncouth, Jerk Haus.

2. JW House on the Wakenitz; first white house from left

3. JW House with Bull Durham in upper window

Home it would be – at least for a while. We grabbed our duffel bags and rusty rifles, walked stiffly up the steps, through the heavy oak doors with little oval windows protected by matching ornate iron grates, up two more marble-inlaid steps, and finally entered through a formal vestibule with sliding wooden doors. Ah, warmth at last.

We dropped our duffel bags in the front room of the house, which served as an orderly room, and Bohan quickly took us downstairs to the dampish basement where we locked our trusty and soon to be even more rusty rifles in what passed for an armory. Back upstairs, we were guided past the office and into a large room filled with over-stuffed chairs and oak tables. At one end, a low wooden railing divided the room in two. Two couches and a huge movie screen that pulled down from the ceiling were on the other side of the railing.

4. The perpetual card game

Man, I was taking it all in and still not really believing my eyes, which probably were bugged out to arm's length. Not wanting to seem too awestruck, I glanced at the ceilings way up there, and the windows and doors framed with ornate dark oak woodwork. Immediately to our right was a carpeted staircase leading upstairs. We walked around several guys slouched into soft, stuffed leather chairs arranged around a circular table in front of a quietly burning fireplace. It looked like they were playing pinochle. They nodded politely at us as we opened a double set of tall glass and oak French doors that led into another large room. Here, there were four or five white-clothed tables, several more guys sitting around picking their teeth, and a busty maid, who informed us her name was Karin. I couldn't believe it; we had a maid, for God's sake. I had heard some tales about Lübeck and just laughed them off as typical ASA bullshit, but it seemed they were all true. In fact, the reality seemed better than truth.

Not only that, but to my left, one end of the room, which obviously was the mess hall - er, dining room, was taken up by a huge bar, with a rich deep red-wine-colored oak top and front panels that looked like genuine fake leather vinyl. Behind the bar was a small refrigerator and shelves for booze and glasses. The back wall was painted in dark blue with a decent rendering of some old city monument and Lübecker Bar spelled out in huge Gothic letters.

Well, that was it. Eat, unload, get assigned a room and a room-mate and hit the sheets. Well, not quite. After dinnah, we were summoned to the bar and Bohan began his briefing. This is the dining area you know since you just ate here and it's also used for breakfast and parties and stuff. Just tell the morning maid – her name's Maria - what you want. She doesn't speak English. And she'll usually ask how do you want your eggs? *Rührei oder spiegelei?* Scrambled or sunny-side up? She does understand up. *Mit schinken oder speck?* With ham or bacon? See, you're learning German already. *Kaffee, tee, oder mich.* Coffee, tea, or me. Wait'll you see her, before you answer that one. The little room over there is the maid's hangout, but it also has the dumbwaiter which goes down to the kitchen which is in the basement.

There's food on call almost 24 hours a day, but Chef Böhnlein needs sleep, too. If you treat him right and you're really hungry, he'll let you make your own snacks. I thought, maids and a chef? Unbelievable! This is the Army?

Bohan continued with his spiel, there's not much else downstairs, just a couple of storage rooms and your rifles, of course. Back where you came in and dumped your stuff is the orderly room; there's supposed to be someone on duty at all times there. Lieutenant Bell is the boss for now, at least. That's where you sign out trucks and stuff and get chewed out, if you need it. He's usually not here – I don't know where he hangs out most of the time. The big room you walked through to get here is where we show the movies. The Lübecker Bar you know because you're sitting at it. Here's the tab, keep it honest.

We walked out a glass door leading to a small porch edged with a low thick wall. Turn on the light. Bohan was taking charge. Here's the rear porch. If you walk down the steps, down there, past those weeds and trees – that's the *Wakenitz* - pronounced vah ke nitz - which is a river that turns into a lake as it goes through town. You can swim in it if you want, but it's pretty dirty and right now, it's damn cold. Look past the lake and you can spot the lights from the cathedrals from here. He pointed out a couple boats visible through the trees. A few blocks over to the right, there's a little ferry. Ah, people ferry, you know, a boat that will take you across the lake for a few pfennigs.

This was all spectacular to me, and my mind was storing images away at a million miles an hour; imagine living in a mansion on a lake in the middle of a rather large city – anywhere in the world. That was way beyond my wildest dreams. I vowed to explore the vah ke nitz further – as soon as the weather warmed up.

But for now, it was still frosty outside, so we moved back in the house quickly and made for the stairs, back near the entrance-way. Bohan led the way. Upstairs are the bedrooms – here's yours – he was speaking to me – it's got a balcony overlooking the back yard and the *Wakenitz*. Nice view of the cathedrals, huh? There are more rooms on the third floor, but you don't really want to go up there. Especially not right now. When the doors are closed and you hear squeaking bed springs, it's a pretty good sign you're not wanted in there. Work it out with your room-mate.

5. View from my room

Here's the bathroom. Tub with shower. Don't drink the water. That's pretty much it. Bohan stopped for breath.

I looked inside the bathroom which was much larger than I expected. It was tiled in white with a double green stripe around it. There was a huge bathtub with spray nozzles for showering, a fancy ceramic sink, mirror, and even a foot washer. The wall was defaced in a couple places with the stenciled warning, "Water not safe, do not drink." The toilet was the unusual German type in that yesterday's supper would land on a little platform and then be flushed down the back when you pulled a chain. It was gross and I wondered why this interest in your own body waste? Maybe the Germans liked to check it out to see if they were sick or something; well, whatever, it seemed they were different from Americans in that way. The whole setup was definitely unlike the outhouse I grew up with.

Bohan was finishing up. Keep you room reasonably clean or Elsa the cleaning lady will get pissed. Tomorrow you'll see where you work at the *Blankensee* site and then maybe eat at Mutti's. Mutti's is a little country *Gasthof* – like an inn – it's right next to the site. We've contracted with her for meals so when we're on duty, we don't have to come all the way back here to eat. It's handy and the food is more than decent. Most of the time you'll be eating here, but if you prefer to eat there, that's ok, too. It really doesn't matter. He turned to me as he left. Your room-mate is Mort Weston. He's from Missouri so you know what that means. Be careful what he shows.

Let's see, I thought, a cook, house cleaner, two maids, a bar, a card and movie room, a dining room and a bed room overlooking a lake? That's all? Yes, I answered my own question, and briefly looked heavenwards, that's more than quite enough, thanks. Compared to any place I had ever lived before, this house was, literally, Camelot.

6. From left: Pappy Paine, Al McCrumb. Puffer, Bill LaJeunesse

7. Dick Nelson, Bobby Roark, Willie Landgraf and Maid Karin

8. Pouring a fine cup of hot chocolate at the Niederegger Café

Richard Phegly:

"This NCO at Rothwesten was a real prick and I was elected to crap in his bed. I did the dastardly deed on his sheets and wiped off using his pillowcase then remade his bed. He came in around 1 a.m. and slid into bed then slammed his door and ran to the showers. I fell out of my bed laughing so hard. Word got out that I may have done this deed and I was summoned to the orderly room and questioned by the 1st Sgt. and the CO. They asked and said that they had heard that I did the deed and I was going to be severely punished for doing that to an O. I said I did not do it and if they thought I did it "could they fingerprint it?" The CO told me to get the hell out of his office and a few days later I was shipped off to Lübeck as punishment. Upon arriving at Lübeck I was met at the Lübeck bahnhof by some guys I think Beagle and Landgraf in a vehicle and taken to Jerk House fed dinner and we sat down at a table with 8 cases of beer and I was welcomed to Lübeck. I was poured into a bed at Zwingli house across town sometime during the night. My months in Lübeck were the greatest of my time in the Army. Other than an occasional trouble I was led into, it was great."

The day after our arrival, we newks were herded into a three-quarter ton truck and driven down *Ratzenberger Allee* and onto a narrow lane to our new place of employment for the foreseeable future. However, due to hunger pangs and the clock on the wall, we definitely had to eat first. So we backed up to the *Fliegerhorst Gasthaus*, unofficially known as Mutti's.

Mutti's food was far above the tasteless mess hall chow we had become accustomed to inhaling. I instantly fell in love with the sizzling hot *wienerschnitzel* smothered in green peas, with a few dozen fried potatoes on the side. Frau Else Kruger, better and only known as Mutti, which means mother, in German, was a hearty hausfrau that ran this little inn. Complete with gas pumps, rooms for rent and a small restaurant, it was conveniently located near the turn-off into the field where our little supposedly-secret listening post was situated.

9. Mutti's Gasthaus; recent photo

Mutti's was more than just a place to eat, but also a place to party, recover, and just plain hang out and drink. For some, it also served as an actual home away from home with the gentle Mutti clucking over "her" Ami's like a brooding hen. She served a fine meal, and for some, the thick, brown, *ochsenschwanz suppe* (ox-tail soup) was the epitome of delicious.

10. Hanging out. From left: Mike Raphael, Billy Henderson,
Frank Petinato, Mutti and two unknown linguists

The restaurant sure wasn't fancy, but plain beige walls,
curtained windows, a *zigaretten* machine and separate tables
with tablecloths beat any mess hall I ever ate in. Strange, though,
I never saw any Germans in there. Well, maybe a few. Very few.

11. Inside Mutti's with Mutti; photo by Dick Strader

CHAPTER 3: The "secret" site at Blankensee:

Our little radio site we just called "the site." It was out in the country several miles south and just a bit east of Lübeck and apparently near the *Blankensee*. I say apparently because I was told there is a lake just past the site but I never saw it nor was curious enough to look for it.

The site itself was not much to look at. It was located in a large flat field, which is the standard terrain for northern Germany, and was a rectangular compound that measured approximately 70 yards wide and 175 – 200 yards long – like a stretch football field. It was surrounded by an earthen dike, technically a berm, about six feet tall and topped with weeds, fence and barbed wire. One rickety padlocked gate, which we had to open and close ourselves, let us in – or out. Running just inside the berms that enclosed the area were two narrow concrete roads that split the site length-wise. Between these roads, which supposedly were taxiways for Luftwaffe fighter planes during WWII, the compound was divided into sections by several earthen berms that were perpendicular to the outer berms. I was told this was where the Luftwaffe had parked their planes and the dikes kept more than one or two at a time from being strafed or bombed into little bitty pieces. The planes could taxi down the two concrete paths along the edge of the compound, then take a hard right or left and park in relative safety between the dirt piles. It didn't seem there was enough room for airplanes between the berms, or else they were midget racers. I noticed that the taxiways also led away from the site, and I suspected that there were more airplane parking lots in the nearby woods and our site, with its rows of earthen berms, was the fuel storage area. For all I knew, these berms were burial mounds from some ancient civilization that liked to arrange things in neat rows. The precursors of today's Germans. No one really bothered to look into the matter and it certainly didn't bother me. It just made for a handy place to do our business.

An asphalt runway, which was huge and undiscovered and unscarred during the entire war, was across the road from Mutti's. It was something like 100 yards wide and at least a half mile long because it was also used to launch several gliders at a

17

time in a wide tandem. Its huge size questioned the eyesight of our WWII photo reconnaissance people.

Scattered around the compound were various olive drab deuce and a half trucks with the standard boxy communication huts on the back. These huts were actually fully equipped rooms that simply slid into the steel cargo area of the truck. They were large enough so two or three men and their equipment could work in relative comfort. I say relative because in the winter these things turned into giant refrigerators, and in the summer, they became ovens that would have done the Nazi's proud. There were also several smallish canvas-covered rounded, quonset-like huts, technically known as Jamesways, but just called quonsets or huts by most of us. What did we know? The ground was littered with thick electrical and antenna cables.

12. Comm Center; courtesy of GB Harry Walthall

Sort of central was the comm center, made up of several boxy huts linked together. Off to the side and away from these structures were several large gasoline tanks and a wide parking place to change oil and repair trucks and jeeps. At the far end of the compound was a hut containing a huge diesel generator and behind that, one skinny radio tower about a hundred feet tall and a few shorter ones.

Our site looked like a dump; in fact it was truly a dump; an old Luftwaffe fuel storage dump.

I was ushered into one of the huts situated between the first pair of berms, and found it actually was insulated and even had some sort of smelly kerosine stove. Inside was a double rack of fancy Collins radio sets, which were similar to the ones we had used at Rothwesten. They were made in Cedar Rapids, Iowa, about a hundred miles from my home town. I always found this funny, since after I got kicked out of college, I had applied for a job there and had been turned down. These high-powered state-of-the-art radios would be manned by two more-or-less wide awake 058 dit-takers 24 hours a day 365 days a year. Actually, Christmas was sort of hit and miss.

Our schedule, which may seem like it allowed an inordinate amount of rest, was actually quite brilliant. Copying Morse code for several hours a day is mentally exhausting work and we worked hard and we worked a lot. The ASA was smart enough to realize that time off was necessary in order to avoid burn-out and to keep each 058 relatively fresh and mentally prepared.

Each trick, or daily work schedule, would last eight hours, and we would work three days, take one day off, work three swings, four to midnight, take one day off, then three mids, which lasted from midnight to eight and then take four days off. What we could do during those four days was totally up to us. We could sleep, screw, get drunk, play cards, go to Paris or Copenhagen or Hamburg, read a book or just hang out. The time was ours. It was well understood by all that we had to be ready to start our next shift in fighting condition.

There really wasn't much new to learn here, so the visit was short. We could explore the rest of the site more thoroughly on our own, but we were reminded just how secret our work was supposed to be because we were not invited into any of the other huts; in fact we were told loud and clear that what goes on in those other huts is none of your damn business.

I eventually learned that there were many other sites up and down the East German border that no one talked much about including a direction-finding site in the middle of a moor near *Krummesse* just a few miles from our site. Although the rest of the US Forces were kept away from the border, we had to be as close as possible to the enemy, so our sites were often virtually smack dab on the border.

Wow! I realized with a jolt, were we secret or what! At the very least, due to our position, and the thousands of Russian and East German troops just a few miles away, we were truly expendable.

13. Site; photo by Duain Shaw

Bob Fleming:

The detachment actually came into existence some time prior to '55. When I first got there we didn't have any cryptography. Only voice and morse code guys. Cryptographers came, I believe, in the spring of '56. Same time that we got our first officer. We really had a good group of guys. If you weren't good you could be banished to Bahrdorf which was outside Helmstadt and operated between March and the end of October. It was quite different from Lübeck. You lived in tents and had a GI mess tent, etc. Nobody wanted to get transferred there from Lübeck. We spent weekends and three day passes in Copenhagen, Amsterdam, and Hamburg. (Der Reeperbahn) We built the bar at J-Haus and usually had a party there on Saturday night. Managed to get some local combos who wouldn't charge much if anything. We, of course, supplied the beer and booze. Lübeck was one helluva place.

Mort Weston:

"Most of the time the old WWII vehicles we had would not run and Pappy, the motor pool wizard, at one time had only one 3/4 ton truck to transport us back and forth to work. It would only run on two or three of the four cylinders and jumped down the road as the German people laughed at us passing by them.

The German border guards had new military vehicles and it seemed to rub something inside of me each time they would pass our olive jumping goose.

The Rothwesten HQ did not provide cooks for us at Lübeck but they did give us a basic assistance subsidy of $77.10 each month to buy our meals. We ate a lot of sandwiches, junk, milk and liquor purchased on our Bremenhaven Px runs. The food was left out day and night in the kitchen as one trick would arrive and another would leave Jürgen-Wullenwever-Str. 10. The nutrition was bad, many of the guys would not take the time to go to town or find a restaurant nearby. A lot of them could not order food since they could not speak the language. Liquor became the only source of vitamin C. Scurvy started in some of the agents and we were taken to Hamburg to be checked by English doctors. Someone came up with the idea that we should pool our BAS money and Class 5 or 6 liquor cards to hire a cook and maids and so we drove to Bremerhaven to get a complete stock of booze for the bar and hired a bartender. Drinks were put on a monthly tab or paid with army script. James Bruce, an 058, was our first treasurer. He paid all bills and our hired personnel and at the end of each month we all split the remaining pot. I managed to save after Jim's management about $1500 dollars and also as the Germans say, "Live like God in France".

Not only were there intercept and direction-finding sites scattered around the area but the men who manned them were also scattered around Lübeck. Most of the language guys stayed at Zwingli 8, another house in a fine neighborhood sort of across town and others, who may have been on short-term (TDY) assignments or were waiting for a room to open up at JW *Strasse* or Zwingli, often stayed in various apartments and hotels, such as the *Reuterkrug* or a place on *Rathenaustrasse*. Our Lt. stayed in his own apartment around the corner from JW *Strasse*.

CHAPTER 4: Lübeck; The Neighborhood

My very first ride back from the site to our little house on *Jürgen-Wullenwever Strasse* gave me some time to reflect. I knew I could handle the work, after all, how hard was it to copy morse code? It was pretty routine by now, but all the other stuff - the booze, the free time, the girls, the maids and a chef, for God's sake - that was another story, and no doubt about it, it was all new to me and I had a lot to learn. But I wasn't really sure I wanted to learn about everything.

I hopped out of the truck and trotted upstairs; it was time to unpack, and see what Mort my room-mate looked like in the daylight. He was a true, decent, down-home Missouri boy, whose real name was Marion, but because he once worked in a mortuary in order to get prepped for medical school, got hung with the nickname, Mort. He helped me get my stuff relatively organized, and then walked me through the neighborhood. Right next door was a church, apparently Catholic, since there were some nuns standing around, and on the other side of our house was a rather nicely turned-out manse, undergoing extensive renovation. Walking down the sidewalk, back towards town, we turned the corner onto *Moltkestrasse*, where there was a handy little store, selling milk, beer, candy, a few groceries, *zigaretten*, and other unimportant necessities and an *Imbiss* for snacks.

14. The corner sch*nell Imbiss*

There was also a tram stop with such a long name, a *Strassenbahnhaltestelle,* that it nearly took a whole sign post by itself. Attached was a handy schedule, which meant we could hop on a street car and be downtown or almost anywhere else in Lübeck in minutes. Sometimes more.

During my initial expedition to the store, I discovered that our area of Lübeck was heavily populated by little kids – tons of kids, from maybe eight to thirteen years old, indicating that their parents were completely recovered from the war and getting on with repopulating the country - apparently as fast as possible. These little hopes for the future liked to follow us down the street, begging for chocolate or chewing gum. It is universally known and obviously part of little kids gene structure that GI's are suckers for kids. These Jünglings weren't from poor families, but they certainly knew how to beg. I think they had a built-in advanced early-warning radar system, because one minute the street would be empty and the next second, you would be swarmed by kids begging and pleading for *"Kaugummi, bitte,"* or *"Schokolade?"*

15. Me and my gang on a neighborhood milk run

Luckily, I soon found they were good humored, since it didn't seem to matter if they got any chewing gum or chocolate or not. I could imagine that two dozen little kids could pretty much bury a guy through their sheer force of numbers, like a swarm of sharks around a piece of raw *wienerschnitzel*. Mort and I continued our tour, and the swarm petered out as we walked back past our house, past the church, and through a well manicured park to the little ferry that would chug us across the Wakenitz to yet another park and the local Opel car dealership.

So this was our neighborhood; a broad street, quiet, tree-lined, flower garden bedecked, and certainly more opulent than anywhere I had ever lived before. It was definitely not your typical army base, and I was sure I could get used to this.

How could American soldiers end up in such fine quarters? Various stories of the origin of our good fortune were around, but it seems our houses were either leased or appropriated from the German government, the British, or private German citizens. Take your pick. Whatever the case, the houses had to be big enough to handle at least a dozen rambunctious troopers. Our house was fine, but the house next door, #12, was even finer.

16. Neighborhood gang!

17. Neighborhood princess

18. Neighborhood three-wheeled van

Bob Fleming:

The two houses on JürgenWollenwever Strasse were owned by the British. In the Spring of '56, Pete Hetherington and I moved in with the British in the house that was next to JW #10. The British house was occupied by two or three British civilians who conducted some sort of operation in Lübeck. The house was quite lavish. Pete and I had rooms on the third floor. As I recall we were staying there because there was some plan in the works for our Detachment to take over the place when the British moved out. If the British left and there weren't any Americans in the house the property would revert to the German Govt.

Pete and I could never figure out what the Brits were doing. There was a guy named Val, who looked (and operated) like Errol Flynn. He was probably in his mid to late forties. He had a secretary who was probably in her fifties. They had a butler, cook and driver. Their car was a VW Beetle.

When I met these guys, they had upgraded to a Cadillac convertible. Occasionally, if we were good, they would let us ride to the beach with them. They had an extremely good life.

19. The neighborhood British agents of some sort

CHAPTER 5: The Riverboat!

20. The fabulous Riverboat

The day turned into twilight, which, since we were up so far north, lasted a long time in Lübeck, and I had a full stomach and loads of curiosity. Time to get dressed – civvies, only, please - and head downtown. When we were off-duty, we were under strict orders not to be seen gamboling around town in any sort or part of an Army uniform. The more invisible we were, the better. This was supposed to keep up the pretense of secrecy, since Lübeck was definitely located in the British zone of control.

Four of us piled into someone's little Opel, and soon we were looking for a *parkplatz* near the *Holstentor*, which is Lübeck's remaining city gate from the 15th century. One quick look and I realized that this was the old building painted on the wall behind the Lübecker Bar; it turned out to be the city symbol imprinted on everything from underwear to outerwear. However, that night no one really cared about the hallowed *Holstentor*, as our mission was entirely something else. We parked, walked a block, came to a canal bridge, took a left down a flight of concrete stairs, curved around a wide sidewalk, and there before our eyes, tied and firmly bolted to the shore was, we were told, a true ship of dreams, the glorious and magnificent Riverboat!

Actually, it was a run-down old barge, but that didn't really matter. A crowd was already gathering, waiting for the doors to open and promptly at eight o'clock, a steady line of eager customers surged gingerly up a narrow gangplank and into the bowels of the former pride of somebody's barge fleet. What a blast this was going to be! They didn't have anything like this back in Cedar Falls. A quick check-in by the bouncer and a d-mark *oder zwei* for a ticket and we were in. It was filling up fast – luckily with girls and not with water – and a quick look around in really dim lights showed a long, low room with a small dance floor close by and, way down at the far end, what looked like a bar and another small dance floor. However, strangely, in the darkness the most noticeable thing was a gaping hole in the middle of the floor.

Further inspection showed that the hole was surrounded by a pipe railing and actually opened to the hold down below, which was now a dance floor surrounded by candle-lit tables. The Riverboat had two floors; it was possible to sit upstairs at a table around the railing and watch the dancing below or sit below and see practically nothing. It was crowded already. It was dark and this was absolute perfection.

My heart was beating the proverbial mile a minute at this absolutely new experience. We made our way down the narrow aisle on the right, passed up a few tables and sat down at the bar. Here, we were on high stools and had the freedom to look around in all directions. I calmed down enough to order a Coke, pronounced correctly in German, Coke ah, and turned around to take in every morsel of the scene. The opening to the hold below was about 10 feet wide and 35 to 40 feet long. At the far end where we had come in, a slick wooden slide provided for a quick and abrupt and more often than not, embarrassing, grand and maybe sore entrance to the dance floor below.

Half-way down the length of the hold on our right was a platform that measured approximately eight by ten feet and was slightly lower than our floor level. A quartet was tuning up. I was surprised to see an all-black jazz band that seemed out of place in lily-white and genetically selected Germany. But it turned out these guys were from Saint Louis and could they play! Without warning they burst full-bore into the "Muskrat

Ramble" and it seemed the boat shifted slightly - at least my heart jumped three feet - and suddenly the place was electric. Electric jazz. This was Lübeck and I was here!

It was awesome. I mentally moved my heart back into place, swallowed hard, and looked slowly around. It was time to check out the chicks. Actually, I was petrified. My experience with girls was pretty much nil. I had a crush or two in high school, but because I lived an extra-long seven miles from the town where my school was located, and my only transportation was a leaky old 1929 Model A Ford with a top speed of 35 miles per hour, I had very little opportunity to actually talk to a girl, much less touch one. I didn't even make it to our junior and senior proms, that's how bad it was.

Coming from a town of about 95 people, with a strict Dutch conservative religious background, I was totally intimidated by the girls from the big city of over 2000. In most worldly things, including the ASA, Naïve was my middle name. Whatever the reason, right at this moment I was truly terrified. I think my ass bones were actually trying to grow thorny little spicules into my bar stool. I could look around and see all the eager flesh and blood and available young ladies, most of them really quite attractive. My body wouldn't move, but at least my mind was active.

Although I had a brief indoctrination to the opposite sex, I wasn't quite comfortable in their presence. Back during my two thirds of a year in college, before I got kicked out for throwing a garbage pail up and over and on top of a flag pole, a couple of my room-mates physically dragged me to dance lessons in the Commons, and I eventually learned the two-step and how to jitterbug. Patti Page. But that was completely structured and controlled; here the music was wild, loud, and the trumpet and the beat went right though you. Electric jazz – live and not through some damn tinny jukebox speakers and I loved it. I just couldn't move.

A tall, good-looking brunette, holding a cigarette like, you know, how they hold them in the movies, slid up to one of the guys, I think his name was Puffer, and he whispered something in her ear. She nodded, smiled, doused her cigarette and came directly over to me. Oh man, time actually did seem to stand still

29

as she floated in graceful slow motion toward me. "Come," she said, "my name is Uschi. Let's dance." She grabbed my hand and pulled me off the stool and down a narrow circular staircase to the dance floor on the lower level. She was strong and determined and instead of my behind, now my tongue seemed somehow attached to the bar stool, for I didn't say a word of protest. What was there to talk about? And anyway the music was way too loud for conversation.

The hold was really packed, hip to butt, and she held out her arms and I grabbed them gingerly like the gentleman I was, and the music slowed as we began to sway together. Not exactly like the way I thought dancing was supposed to be, but it was better than anything I had ever been taught. This was dancing – real dancing. We were more than cheek to cheek and I noticed a certain delicate part of my body begin to respond to her movement. She noticed, too, and smiled up at me and said something I couldn't hear. What a great way to dance. And I was just a beginner!

The music stopped and I began to walk stiffly off the dance floor, but she pulled me back as the ensemble burst into something loud and fast again. Time to jitterbug - or at least to try, since it was so jammed that it was pretty difficult to tell who was dancing with whom. As the army would say, "nothing but elbows and assholes," but that was ok, too. This music really got to you. I could learn to like this, too.

The jitterbugging calmed my turgid body part to a more controlled state, and with the band already out of breath and starting a break, we worked our way back up the stairs to the bar. I held her hand. The guys were grinning, I was grinning and I believe Uschi was, too. I turned her back over to the guy who had set me up. Later, I found out she was sort of the resident easy-lay to a large share of the guys in the detachment, but what the hell – she was my first real dance to a real live band and she was terrific and she was a sweetheart and I'll never forget her. She gave me confidence that I could actually deal with the opposite sex without totally embarrassing myself.

I was to find out very soon that this skill was highly necessary in life.

21. Interior of the good ship Riverboat

The Riverboat turned out to be the central place for the social activities of many of us Lübeckers – both the North American kind and the local natives. You could go there to get drunk, to dance, to just listen to the music, to socialize, to pick up a girl – and they were plentiful – or take an actual date, which seemed like bringing a sandwich to a banquet. Many young ladies came down to Lübeck from Denmark and Sweden on holiday, but more often than not, they came down to get laid. Well, not solely for that purpose since I'm sure that there were plenty of sturdy young Vikings available for that purpose back home. Maybe it was just to get laid by someone from a different country. Maybe it was to just get the hell out of the house for a while. Whatever the reason, they were plentiful in and around Lübeck, the Riverboat, and even at our house. The sexual appetite of the Danish girls became well know throughout our detachment. Some of the guys went up to Copenhagen for their first break and never went anyplace else from that time on. To top it off, most of these Scandinavians spoke better English than we did.

That first night in the Riverboat was a revelation. I could dance; I could actually converse with a girl; I found that I must have had a certain attraction to the opposite sex, since everyone I asked to dance agreed readily and some even asked me. I never thought of myself as attractive, but I was relatively big, being nearly six feet three inches tall and weighing about 180 pounds. I heard some girls describing me as "*niedlich*." Cute. How can someone this big be cute? Well that was me, I guess and whatever it was, it made me a chick magnet.

Apparently I was not magnetic enough, for as the hour approached one a.m., emptyhanded, we made a quick run through *Der Kahn*, across the bridge from the Riverboat. However, the scene at *Der Kahn* was quiet and it was virtually empty. It certainly didn't live up to its reputation as the place to go. Now, apparently, it was the Riverboat's turn to shine. So we all piled back into the Opel and made our way back to *Jürgen-Wullenwever Strasse* with only our tired bodies to show for it. We were, after all, working men, and some of us had to be out at the *Blankensee* site by eight. Young bodies fortunately, can take a pretty good beating. Mine was exhausted, but happy.

22. Der Kahn, the Riverboat's older sister

Anonymous for a reason:

Me and a couple buddies were hanging out at the Riverboat one night and I guess I got a little too drunk. They had burning candles on the tables down in the hold and you could use them to write your name or draw dirty pictures on the ceiling with the candle smoke. Well, I must of gotten carried away, because I was trying to set the tablecloth on fire with a candle and some big German dude knocked me halfway across the floor. He was really pissed and I was lucky we didn't get into a fight. He probably would have kicked the crap out me. But thinking back, I was totally stupid. I could have set the whole damn boat on fire and with the set up there with no emergency exits, there would have been me and about 200 other charred bodies floating in the canal. I have been grateful ever since for that big German dude. I wish I could thank him.

23. View from north window, J Haus

CHAPTER 6: The Girl in Leather Gloves

Days passed quickly. With our screwy schedule, learning how to sleep at all times of the day was high on the list of things to do. Plus I had to get my room in shape, and more importantly learn how to play liar's dice at the Lübecker Bar. This game ended with the loser having to chug his beer or coke and cognac, and since I wasn't much for drinking, it didn't take me long to turn into a spectator.

I was a little short on civilian clothes and being the good soldier, I made my way downtown to the *Karstadt* to buy a German sport coat. After trying on a few I ended up with a black wool single-breasted three-button jacket with teeny purple dots. Wearing this, I figured I could blend in with the locals a bit better and, besides, I liked it. When I went out, it was usually wearing gray slacks, a white or nearly white shirt and maybe a cheap knit tie and that god-awful sport coat, which eventually got borrowed by about half-dozen guys. I'm sure they hoped my chick magnetism would rub off. I just wanted it returned clean.

Despite my new confidence discovered at the Riverboat, I found out that not everyone thought I was perfect. At the *Karstadt*, Lübeck's premier department store, when I went to buy my sport coat, I flipped over this really cute girl, with a perfect heart-shaped face, a brilliant smile, gorgeous legs - what I could see of them behind the counter - and a trim, shapely figure. I immediately began to pant and followed her around like a little puppy. Her name tag read "Helga," and she worked in the leather glove department and during the next couple weeks I must have tried on at least five hundred pairs of gloves. Unfortunately, she couldn't speak one single word of English, and I only spoke enough German to make a complete fool of myself. I was persistent, and I tried to invite her out a dozen times, but nothing came out right. Just by accident, one day on my way to the *Karstadt,* I saw her walking all cozy-like with a big handsome German stud. I was shot down, smashed, crashed and burned, and for a long time afterward, whenever I smelled leather, I thought of her.

CHAPTER 7: Baptism Under Fire, Part I

24. *Clemenstrasse;* photo by Dick Strader

One night around midnight, someone ran screaming into the house on *Jürgen-Wullenwever Strasse.* "Bobby's getting the shit kicked out of him by a bunch of Polish sailors down on *Clemenstrasse,"* he babbled, "we've gotta go and help him." So the biggest guys around, which included me, piled into Mr. Excitable's car and headed down toward what constituted part of Lübeck's waterfront area, the infamous, *Clemenstrasse.* I had heard the guys talking about it a lot. It was the red light street of Lübeck and not a particularly nice place to be late at night.

I was about to get my baptism under fire and, frankly, I wasn't too thrilled. In fact, I was scared shitless and wondering, who the hell was Bobby and why am I obligated to help rescue this fool? If he kept his dumb ass out of there, he wouldn't be getting pounded into little pieces. As we hurtled recklessly down the bumpy streets on our heroic mission, my fear dissipated somewhat when I realized that whatever was going on was probably over by now. And that, indeed, turned out to be true.

There was a crowd of people still milling around and luckily for Bobby, about four or five of Lübeck's finest were on the scene. He was bloodied, but not seriously hurt, and someone was loading him into a tiny Austin Healy sports car and heading for home. I breathed a gigantic sigh of relief, and someone suggested that now that we're down here, let's get a drink. We walked past a couple bars and finally settled for one about halfway down the street, which really wasn't that big. Inside, it was smoky and dirty and someone was trying to stuff marks into a creaky old juke box. I was reminded just a little of the Commons back in college! There actually was a bar and several men were standing around drinking and chatting. I could see why. One look at the "girls" and I almost retched. Wrinkled, downright ugly, half-naked, pathetic old crones with makeup encrusted faces and bright red lipstick were sitting around in what I suppose they thought were alluring poses. The most visible part of their body was their crotch and that, like the rest of their offerings, was not a pretty sight!

I wondered, what the hell were good clean-living all-American boys doing hanging out with the likes of these? My God, now I could understand why some of the guys drank so much. If this was a sample of their love life, then they were really in trouble. I couldn't believe that they actually paid for this? It seemed damn disgusting to me. Maybe there were some young, beautiful whores around, but I didn't see any evidence of that. I decided that was it for me. If Bobby and anyone else wanted to come down here and fight over some smelly old whores with a bunch of drunken Polish sailors, from now on, that was his problem, not mine. It's time to go home, I insisted. To each his own. We left.

25. *Clemenstrasse* photo; 2001, nothing changes

Jack Weber:

We, the fighting '69ers, drank well, ate well, frolicked well, traveled well, and did our jobs well. We covered our assignment for ol' Uncle Sam first class. From the HQ on Jurgen-Wollenwever Strasse to the Blankensee Huts to the summer test projects at Dahme, Groemitz and Fehmarn, the 319th was the best.

To our credit, we always came to the aid of our boys in trouble! Always! Many times the locals tried their hands at challenging the "Amis." Yes, the "Amis" accounted for themselves very well when called upon. The Blau Maus, the July 4 Strasse Battle, Jedermans, St. Pauli Bar, plus numerous other jousts were matters tended to in prompt and proper order by the rank and file of Company B of the Three-one-nine!

One night, a frantic phone call call came to Jerk Haus. Our hero, "Fatty" Gemmell, was in trouble at Jedermans. (Nothing new here.) So we proceeded again to rescue our Artie. The fire brigade responded and quickly saved the day (along with the big-ones rotund ass).

And more tale of the tape from Jack Weber:

Please be aware that the day following the July 4th incursion on the Street of Dreams, our everlovin' 319th motorpool/supply sergeant, Jimmy Shaw, drew the assignment to drive me (the wounded lion) north to the base hospital in Todendorf. He proceeded, without compassion, to drag my bloody and battered body along, as I recall, behind his jeep.

Because I was unable to escape unscathed from that hellish strasse altercation, it was off to see the U.S. Army type doctor. The official diagnosis was a broken nose and four broken ribs. Whoops! Thank the man upstairs that there was no major damage done to my face. Who cares about about a nose? (Lieber Gott, what would the girls of Lübeck have done if the wonderous Hulk were disfigured)? Those little Kraut somebitches used me for a very large soccer ball. As God is good, a 300 lb. hooker with whom I had an ongoing platonic friendship *in house #1B saved my tight little derriere that night by tossing off those Germanic tribesmen, one by one, from my weakened form. At the time, they said there were a dozen of them, but I counted at least 200. You know, I always liked that large lady. She definitely resembled our compadré Artie Gemmell. Ok, so she weighed a little less than he did but she was one hell of a lot better looking.*

Entrance to C-Strasse; photo by Jim Miller

Pat Moyna:

In my case, the introduction to Clemenstrasse was literally the first day (night actually). Billy Pass and I made the long trip from Rothwesten with Dennis Butler in his VW Microbus when we were reassigned from the 184th. We arrived in the city around 6:00 PM and it was dark. We went to a nice restaurant in the InnenStadt and got a bite before looking for the site.

None of us had a clue where it was and nobody at the restauran volunteered any info. When we paid up, we asked the Ober where the Americans were located. He looked at us like we were Martians and said "There are no Amerikaners in Lübeck!"

We were confused and wondered if we had gone to the wrong Lübeck (like there was another). Anyway we decided we could find it ourselves and started driving around. We asked at a gas station and several pedestrians and got the same answer. By now it was 8 o'clock and we were getting concerned. So we started just driving around looking for USAREUR plates. We didn't realize that the Untertrave was circular and made the loop 3 or 4 times before we noticed a lot of the scenery looked the same. We decided a good person to ask would be a cabbie since they haul the drunks home and so we tried a couple, but they didn't seem to know much either.

Finally we spotted a GI plate and of course it was parked right at the mouth of Clemenstrasse. We parked and walked up the street to see if we could spot the GIs but they were nowhere in sight. It didn't take long to figure out where we were but at least people there would know where to find Amis.

We finally found a cabbie there who said he knew and gave us directions. They weren't very good and it took more than an hour and more stops before we found Blankensee Str.,where our regular Army barracks had been built. By the time we got in, it was around 10:30 and we were whipped.

We signed in with the CQ and he told us to go to the basement club for a beer while he tried to find us a place to sleep for the night. He bunked us in rooms of guys on leave and in the morning we made more permanent arrangements. It was a memorable experience.

CHAPTER 7 1/2: Baptism Under Fire, Part II

One Saturday night, slightly chilly, I was invited out to a party in what was supposed to be a popular little *gasthof* in some little no-name village just outside Lübeck. I hopped in a car and a bunch of us rode out on dark, unlit streets. It didn't take me long to realize I had no idea where we were. No matter. It wasn't really a party party, but just a chance to mix with the local females, listen to a loud German band, dance, and for many of the guys, to get dead drunk. I was relishing my new-found interaction with the opposite sex, dancing with many different partners, but one in particular, whose name got lost in the noise, seemed to have her eye on me. After several dances, getting closer and tighter, it was obvious she had more than her eyes on me, as, maybe for the first time, I noticed that this was a girl that was more than amply endowed in the breast area and was totally into squeezing them against my body as much as possible.

Not only that, but her breasts were hard. Rock hard. And I thought the feminine body was supposed to be soft and supple. And girls were supposed to be passive. I had a lot to learn, for here was a wildly frisky young *fräulein* with her arms wrapped tightly around my neck and seeming intent on drilling her steel-tipped boobs clear through my chest. I wasn't quite sure of the next step, since there was so much noise, shouting, and occasional off-key singing going on that it was impossible to concentrate. I just kept dancing. However, my lower appendage seemed to be responding quite well on its own despite the din, and I was beginning to quite thoroughly enjoy the cheek to cheek, chest to chest and pelvis to pelvis contact with this steel-tipped *mädchen*. Even as inexperienced as I was I knew that this rhythmic sensual contact just shouldn't go on in a public place. However, a quick glance around the smoky room assured me that many couples were locked in similar embraces. No wonder this place was so popular.

Everything was going so smoothly, but, what the hell... The next thing I knew someone tapped me on the shoulder, maybe it was Mort, maybe it was someone else, but he said, basically, Hey, Johnss, it's time to go. We got the mid shift. Sure enough, he was right. The clock was winding towards midnight, and we had to get back to town, change clothes and get our hapless butts out to the site. Reluctantly, I unwrapped myself from the iron-breasted *Brünhilde* and turned her over to someone else. She kept right on bumping and humping and probably didn't even notice the difference.

What a night, at least a partial night. If duty hadn't called, I suspect I would have been in for a very special form of education. Instead, it was obvious that someone else was privileged to enjoy the fruits of my evening. No one thanked me, and I never returned to that *gasthof* in that little no-name village somewhere on the edge of town. Not that I knew where it was.

Another form of education happened late one night. I missed the last *strassenbahn* and started to walk across the center of town to JW *Strasse*. About half-way home, on a narrow street just before the bridge over the Trave, a balding, unshaven character popped out of a doorway, grabbed me by the arm and started smacking his lips and babbling in drunken German. I shook him off and continued walking. He followed me, grabbed my arm again and continued smacking his lips. Enough was enough. I shouted, "Raus!" in his face and bent over to pick up a convenient beer bottle. He fled. I walked faster toward home.

26. Ingrid

CHAPTER 8: The Bay of Frozen Dreams

27. The beach

The wet spring slowly evolved into summer, and the gang I was usually with, Bill McMasters, Bill LaJeunesse, Mort Weston, Wes Roach, Alfred McCrumb, Duain Shaw, to name a few major players, started heading northward a few miles to the beaches and bone-freezing waters of Lübecker Bay. This meant *Travemünde,* a huge resort area spreading around the western shores of this frigid bay. These waters are part of the Baltic Sea and even in the early summer, it was possible to chill your beer and anything else in them.

A huge casino dominated the skyline above the main beach, but it was too rich for our blood and anyway it was heavily populated by those of the older generation. Which to us, meant, too boring. Way too boring.

Visible far across the bay the shore was East Germany. It was bare. Through one of the pay-per-view binoculars mounted on the sidewalk every 100 yards on so, you could see there were no houses, no resorts, no people; nothing except an occasional lonely soldier on patrol with his trusty East German Shepherd and a small gray patrol boat, putzing back and forth just off the deserted beach. They were there, ostensibly, to keep us from invading them because no one in their right mind would try to swim across that bay. The bay of frozen dreams.

At *Travemünde strand*, or beach, it seemed that virtually no one ever went swimming. I tried it once for about ten seconds and that was it. There was a great broad sand beach that would do Jamaica proud, but most people seemed quite content simply to lay out of the wind in a wicker *cabanà*, or else keep their blood warm by building their version of a tall wind-blocking *Neuschwanstein* castle. It was also fun watching little kids who dared to venture a few feet into the water turn blue. Much time was also spent out and out ogling each other; but forget swimming, it was just too damn cold.

There was plenty of sand, plenty of drink, and there were plenty frisky young fräuleinin and nordic queens to eyeball. I learned only one phrase in Swedish, but it was a good ice-breaker. It was pronounced svens fleeka, and when spoken as a question meant, "Swedish girl?" and that was enough to get an answer - usually in English, since those two words told them I was no Norseman.

Most of these chance meetings ended up with little to show for it except a sunburn. We knew these girls were here for only a few days, so long-lasting relationships were difficult to foresee; and besides, there were plenty of Lübecker fräuleinin to go around. There were only a few of us hot-blooded Americans up here, and Lübeck had a population of 100,000 which were excellent odds in any nationality.

28. Three and a half beauties. (Note girl on far right

29. *Travemünde* promendade

30. *Travemünde* beach scene; Waiting

31. Casino at *Travemünde* during filming of movie

32 . *Travemünde* beach ball

Most of us saw plenty of Scandinavian girls that we would, obviously, like to court – or whatever. In our eyes, they were all drop-dead gorgeous blondes or almost blondes, but deep down we knew that this was not the same scene as the Riverboat and these girls were probably unattainable. Not being too smart, we figured, what the hell, it wouldn't hurt to try. One girl, named Inge, from Stockholm, I was chatting up most of one afternoon, and we laughed and had fun and arranged to meet again the next day, same time, same place. She was, without a doubt, one of the most beautiful females I had ever seen, especially in a bathing suit; tall, slender, long blonde hair, great chest, tanned, and seemingly eager. She was a true Nordic dream.

I left to hunt up the guys that had to be at work on the swing shift and about an hour later, just by chance, as we were driving out of town, I saw her pull up in front of the Casino restaurant in a big shiny new Mercedes with German license plates and a handsome middle-aged guy that definitely was not acting like her father. That ended my Scandinavian rhapsody in a big hurry. I was hurt, angry, and frustrated and swore off women for at least several hours. I realized I wasn't in the same league as Mr. Mercedes and this gorgeous creature belonged in some fashion magazine or on a movie poster or somebody's yacht. That night I talked myself into believing I was better off without her and life must go on. I didn't even try to make the date the next day so I don't know if she showed up. I thought about hiding behind a tree to check, but instead, I just let the matter drop and stayed away from *Travemünde* that day. It crossed my fuddled mind that it was doubtful that she got stood up too often. With a start, it also crossed my mind that maybe it really wasn't her in that Mercedes.

33. A Nordic queen with queen mother

Experience and a few pointed questions made us realize that many of these young Scandinavian feminine holiday-celebrants were already spoken for back home and were on a last fling before getting married to Leif Ericsson or someone similar.

Still, it seemed they had no qualms about mixing it up with someone old enough to be their grandfather. I wasn't interested in being a sugar daddy and I was too young and poor, anyway. I decided there were just too many other grains of sand on that particular beach to fret about one bad experience.

It didn't take too long to learn that that picking up the opposite sex on the beach was not easy. There were always too many other people around and it was daylight and very bright out and not particularly conducive to romance. People, even young women, had other things on their minds, like sunning themselves, eating, reading and just relaxing. Through trial and too many errors, we discovered that it was best, frankly, to just go to the beach and have fun. Whatever happened, happened.

What eventually evolved was that a bunch of guys that had a day off or were working swings or mids would bring a bunch of Lübeck girls to the beach and party and frolic all day. There really wasn't much pairing up, although that did happen once in a while, but the whole scene was pretty tame. However, if one came off a mid shift, it was not unknown to simply go to the beach and fall asleep. There was more than an occasional fried carcass as no one rotated the hapless sleeper.

Due to the nature of our 24 hour schedules, which caused major sleep problems for some, and due to the fact that we were in the army which was notorious for sending people here or there at a moment's notice, really close friendships between the members of our detachment were few and far between. We all had buddies we hung out with, but this seemed to depend more on who had a car and who had time off to do something.

It was almost like a family thing and we all got along amazingly well. I can't recall one fight or serious argument between us during my entire stay in Lübeck. Perhaps it was simply the magic of the place. Perhaps it was like this in Camelot. Most likely, we all knew if we got into serious trouble with each other we would be packing our bags the next day.

The days at the beach in *Travemünde* were usually calm and just plain old-fashioned fun. Not much changed as the sun went down; it just got slightly darker. For most of us the serious night life on the beach was too expensive – the fancy restaurants, bars, the casino – and we felt too out of place with the big cars, the girls in long formal gowns, for God's sake. Germany was rebounding from the war in a big way, and I think they definitely liked to show it off.

Our idea of night life on the beach was about 180 degrees from that of the typical northern European vacationer. It revolved around a small campfire, a brat or two and a big tub of ice-cold beer, which we had to warm up after taking it out of the Bay. A squawky portable radio would provide the music, and we usually brought our own girls, as well. The quiet fire, the long gentle twilights, and the overall peaceful nature of the moment converted many of our Teutonic brothers and sisters to this genuine American pastime. If any couple got the urge for something more, there were thousands of empty wicker *cabanàs* just begging to be used. They were not for me; I hated them because of a personally embarrassing moment that happened late one night in one of those damned wicker hell holes.

On most Saturday evenings, there was a formal band concert held on the promenade in front of the Casino. It definitely wasn't the jazz band of the Riverboat, but a genuine full-blooded symphony orchestra with violins, oboes, tuxedoes with white gloves and the like. It played to huge crowds and its mixture of show tunes and classical music was well received – it was the *Travemünde* version of the Boston Pops Orchestra. Even for us battle-hardened culture-deprived *soldaten,* it was an unfamiliar but surprisingly pleasant way to spend a few moments in the dusky light.

That particular evening, the tear-drop street lights were just coming on as the sky was turning deep blue and a couple of us were leaning on the concrete balustrade, soaking in the sounds that wafted through a gentle breeze, when, without warning, the orchestra suddenly struck up, "Rock Around The Clock," the Bill Haley and the Comets big hit of the 20th century. The whole beachfront just went nuts, and people started to dance and jump around and sing and clap. So here you had all these middle-aged and up stuffed shirt people, some in tails and gowns, along with their kids and grandkids, just acting like goofy teenagers. It was great and the concert *meister* got a rousing standing ovation since everyone was standing anyway. He also probably got chewed out since I was told it never happened again. For me, though, that was a wonderful moment in time.

34. Hanging out at *Travemünde*

CHAPTER 9: Cars and stripes

35. Bob Keller, Ed Fitchett. Bobby Roark & his Austin Healey

With the constant need to get to the beach at *Travemünde* or to the site for work or just around town, it didn't take long to realize that owning a vehicle would be highly advantageous in many ways. It would be especially nice to have a private moment with a girl, once in a while. Waiting for a lift to go somewhere was tiring and wasted a lot of good time and although public transportation was good in general, the *strassenbahn* usually didn't go where I wanted to go. Gas for us was cheap, about 12 cents a gallon, but the Germans were already paying more than the 20 times that. And those of us with a little larceny in the heart could always go out to the site and siphon a few gallons from a truck or the big gasoline tanks. I went car-shopping.

I came across this beautiful black 1951 Mercedes 170 in absolutely immaculate condition stuck in the weeds of the back row of a used-car dealer clear across town. The Germans worship their cars, and it was nearly impossible to find a bad used car in the whole city. This car, however, was too expensive for my paltry paycheck, so I decided to become a part owner with three others. We dickered and dithered for a few days and eventually bought it.

It had a powerful six-cylinder engine that would prove very expensive to run when compared to the average four-cylinder engine of the smaller Mercedes 150. Simply put, it was a gas hog. That explained while it was sitting undiscovered in the back row, but for us, that was a non-issue. Its big front and rear fenders, sleek running boards, and shiny chrome radiator topped with the Mercedes star, gave off an aura of importance that was un-mistakable.

Inside, it had a burled walnut dash, chromed steering wheel and soft, plush seats. It came complete with front suicide doors – which meant they opened from the front and if they came open while you were driving, their name came true. This car could go like a bat out of hell and was a true joy to drive.

36. My 1/4 Mercedes and me

It was also the reason for the first and only time I got arrested. Lübeck was on the far eastern side of West Germany, in the British zone, and in order to register our vehicles properly, we had to drive clear across northern West Germany to Bremerhaven, which was the main seaport for the U.S. Forces in West Germany. It was a long, tiring drive, since in order to stay on the four-lane autobahn, we had to dip down to Bremen and then cut back up northwest to Bremerhaven. If we went straight across the country side, we would spend hours more driving on tiny little country roads at 7 miles per hour behind some farm tractor.

Bremerhaven was actually an army base as well as a seaport. There it was still strictly S.O.P. (Standard Operating Procedure) and we had to act and dress somewhat decently on our infrequent trips there. Our trucks were sent regularly to load up on groceries for our kitchen and booze for our bar. The lucky guys who drove the trucks could get a genuine American hamburger at the PX or buy a supply of English-language magazines. For those of us unfortunate enough to get sick or catch a dose of the clap, there was a base hospital.

37. Interior, our trusty Mercedes

Our beautiful car didn't have any license plates on it, so the Mercedes had to be properly registered and insured with the U.S. Forces in Germany. A couple of the part-owners and I made the several hours-long trek to Bremerhaven. There was some snafu and for some reason we couldn't get our plates. So we headed back to Lübeck, again driving without any sort of identification on the car. About 20 miles from Hamburg, a little green and white VW bug with two police officers pulled up behind us and turned on its flashing blue lights and screeching obnoxious ou-ah ou-ah siren.

I wondered what the hell's that for? I better get out of the way. I tromped on the gas pedal and left the little VW police car far in the distance. I slowed back down, and shortly the car was back on my tail so I pushed down on the gas and left him in the dust again. I still wasn't sure of what was going on. We kept this up into the outskirts of Hamburg, when I finally decided to pull off the road into a rest-stop cafe for something to drink and to pee.

As we stepped out the car and began to stretch, the little VW, still with its blue lights flashing and loud ou-ah ou-ah-ing came barreling into the truck stop and skidded to a stop beside us. Two *polizei* got out, red faced, embarrassed, pissed, and furious. They promptly hauled us none-to-kindly off to jail in downtown Hamburg.

Led us off is more accurate; it was impossible to actually haul us off since we couldn't all fit in their car. We were instructed to follow them into the city. Apparently, we were being arrested for not having a license plate. We sat in an outer office after identifying ourselves – we were in Army fatigues – and made a call to headquarters at Jurg Haus and, hopefully, to Lt. Jim Bell, our CO. He could have been anywhere from the site to his apartment, but luckily for us he was actually in the orderly room. Not his favorite place. We waited impatiently several hours for him to get there, as he had to borrow license plates from someone's car. When he finally did arrive, he was beyond perturbed. We must have interrupted something real important.

We were relieved to find he wasn't angry at us. He ranted at the police so hard that I began to feel sorry for them, reminding them of who won the war and they damn well better shape up and leave his men alone. We were released, bolted the plates on the Mercedes and fled to a late and cold supper.

We still didn't have our own plates, and in order to keep this fiasco from happening again, we took two cardboard cigarette cartons, cut them apart and screwed them into place. We were shortly driving around town with genuine "Chesterfield" license plates. And they were still on when we drove the Mercedes back to Bremerhaven to get the real thing. No one bothered us, and eventually there were other "Pall Mall" and "Lucky Strike" license plates that served temporarily quite well, thank you.

Unfortunately, with time split between four people, I didn't get a whole lot of use out of this car. One of the other owners, Dave Ade, became my room-mate a bit later. I did take the car into France, though, and it was during a time or political unrest, and we were not supposed to be there.

The French were dallying with communism or at least a strict brand of socialism. It was a time of struggle between right and left that more often than not ended in a riot or its wimpy French equivalent. Americans weren't particularly welcome by the government and many of the populace, as well.

One long break, two other guys and I decided that we were going to drive down to the French Riviera and to hell with any restrictions. We had to get across the border first and that presented quite a problem. Others from our group had tried it without success, as the border and custom guards had strict instructions not to let any Americans out of Germany and into France. It was now a personal thing, a personal challenge to our honor, dignity, and surreptitiousness. It would be the ASA against the world. At least the European world.

Mad Magazine was our favorite choice for serious reading, and this particular month they happened to publish some decal-like stickers with their usual tongue in cheek panache. One of these was shaped like a shield and had a big eagle superimposed on our familiar white stars in a blue field above a red and white striped pattern and the words, "Official United States Taxpayer" circumscribed around the edge. It was verrrry official looking.

We cut this out and carefully stuck it to the lower left-hand corner of the windshield and headed for France. Our clever minds deduced that we should have less trouble going through Luxembourg, as it was still OK to travel there.

South of the city of Luxembourg, any rural border crossing into France would be small and relatively lightly manned. Outwardly calm, I drove this big black Mercedes 170 boldly up to the customs shack, pointed at the "Official United States Taxpayer" sticker on the windshield and behold, the gate lifted. No one even checked our papers. We waved respectfully at the agent and drove with proper stateliness and grace into France. As soon as we were out of sight of the border, though, our gigantic smirking smiles burst into laughter and I almost ran off the road.

We had no trouble with anyone that entire trip and enjoyed ourselves so much that we decided to return as quickly as possible. At that time, we may have been the only Americans in the entire country and going home we went right back to the same crossing into Luxembourg. Stop. Point. Gate up. Drive through. Wave. Crack up. This little fake emblem was a powerful symbol and generally drew a look of respect from everyone who saw it.

That issue of Mad Magazine soon became a collector's item, and impossible to find. I didn't originally think the trick would have worked as well with a less official-looking car, but it didn't seem to matter, as we were shortly putting it on VW's, Austin-Healy's, Opel's and anything reasonably clean that could make it to the border. We used this little Mad Magazine emblem whenever we went to another country; it certainly cut down on waiting time at borders throughout Europe.

My part ownership of a Mercedes was short-lived. A few weeks after our escapade into France, Dave Ade and three of his buddies were going on a week's leave to Belgium – or maybe to France. As they were toodling down the autobahn a few miles southwest of Lübeck at 75 or 80 miles per hour, Dave, who was driving, dropped a lighted cigarette between his legs. While he went fishing for it, he took his eyes off the road and in an instant, the car was hurtling through a low ditch and into an open partially-plowed field.

The car spun around several times while violently rocking from side to side in a serious attempt to roll over. It finally stopped after rolling backward for about a quarter of a mile, with smoke pouring from the engine and exhaust and strange frightening whirring noises coming from the gear box.

There they sat. Four guys stunned and filling their pants. The car was still smoking, and they had to get out or risk being fried. They pushed and kicked, but the doors wouldn't budge. The extreme rocking motion had bent the running boards up so far that they were trapped inside. They were trying to squeeze out of the windows when the farmer who was still plowing part of the field, ran over to see if he could help and stomped the running boards back down.

They all leaped out of the car, but the smoke had stopped when Dave turned the engine off. Looking around, they realized how lucky they had been. In the only place along the entire highway where the ditch was practically flat and there were no trees, posts, cars, trucks or buildings to hit, they ended up turning circles and going backwards in an incredibly soft, freshly plowed field. It had to be the Lübecker Camelot mystique.

The farmer hitched his tractor and towed the car and its four humbled passengers back to the highway. They scraped the dirt off the windows and someone other than still-shaking Dave got behind the wheel. The battered engine fired right up and with an exhibition of Mercedes tradition and reputation, the car proudly managed to clank into gear. They drove straight back to *Jürgen-Wullenwever Strasse*, parked the battered car in front of the house and proceeded to the bar where they began an intense seven-day long drunken binge of thanksgiving. They never left the house for their entire leave.

Shortly thereafter, Dave lost the car to someone from Zwingli House in a poker game and they totaled it against a tree. What a hapless ending for a fine piece of machinery.

Owning one fourth of a car that had been driven backwards in fourth gear for a quarter of a mile didn't make much sense. I sold my share for virtually nothing and bought a used VW. It was a sad parting because that Mercedes was one fine automobile. In any other car we probably would have had four seriously damaged Lübeckers to take care of, or bury.

38. And then I bought My VW

Which I used as a platform for an occasional quick sneak photograph, such as:

39. The Ice Cream twins

CHAPTER 10: Annegret

My little VW Beetle was a completely different vehicle from the Mercedes. It was small, light, underpowered, dangerous, fun to drive, and a great snowplow in the winter. It was nice to be able to just get in and go without checking with someone else. With its cramped leg room and the gear-shift and emergency brake between the seats, the VW was not good for certain mutual exercises between sexes. It made me realize that gear-shift levers moved up and out of the way to the steering column had to be an invention of young horny engineers.

With complete mobility and a blanket in the back seat, I had complete freedom to come and go as I wished. Too often I served as a chauffeur for someone else from our house, since dating as practiced in the USA was unheard of. The Lübeck girls tended to hang in pairs and being alone with a guy was strictly verboten. Maybe it was the culture; maybe it was their parents; maybe they were chicken, but that was an unwritten rule that we had to observe. I got the feeling that any girl who got into this situation too quickly or instantly was considered loose by her fellow citizens – and fair game to the young studly members of our detachment.

The two for one situation could be handled with any creativity, as it was quite simple to drop off number two, while continuing on with number one - unless they were sisters.

I did meet two sisters at the Riverboat. They both were tall, almost six feet, and one, Annegret, was older, a tad bit heavier, nice looking and auburn haired. She had studied and worked in England as an au pair and spoke flawless English with a veddy correct British accent. Her sister, Letta, was a stunning brunette, slim and pretty, and was the one that first caught my eye. She spoke no English, and it soon became obvious that she wasn't interested in learning any, especially from me.

It didn't take me long to find out that settling for number two isn't always that bad. Annegret wasted no time in staking her claim. After dancing most of that very first night with her, she invited me outside for a breath of fresh air. It was cool and it was dark and we ended up panting heavily under the trees and bushes several hundred feet down the canal from the Riverboat.

The sisters lived in a small village some distance from Lübeck and didn't come to town that often. Planning an actual date was difficult and it was like, well, let's try to get together next Saturday. Sometimes she made it to town and sometimes she didn't. When I would see her at the Riverboat, it was sort of a "hey, there's Annegret" type of situation and we made the most of it. We spent more and more time on the canal bank and less and less time inside the boat. Letta was a good little sister and more than willing to leave us alone. After about a month or so of sporadic casual encounters, the direction of our conversations told me that Annegret was priming me for something more serious and I backed off. I didn't intend to be ready for that for quite some time.

We never talked about the future, but Annegret wasn't a quitter. About a month or two after our last dance at the Riverboat, I got a letter from her telling me she would take the bus into town on this certain night and would I be so kind as to meet her on the corner of *Jürgen-Wullenwever Strasse*. This was really quite unusual so I decided to be there at the appointed time. I drove my car down the block and parked under the trees beside the dark street. When she arrived, it turned out she wasn't particularly interested in talking. Within minutes we had the front seats tilted back as far as they could go. It wasn't far enough. We were practically tearing the car apart in our desperation to find any position that would accommodate two rather large people in this tiny VW. The damn steering wheel and the gear shift knob and the foot pedals kept getting in the way. For the first time in my life, I was experiencing the full passion and intensity of an aroused female intent on proving that I was her man and she was my woman.

The car defeated both of us. Bruised and frustrated, I ended up on my knees outside the car. We hadn't spoken two words the whole time. It ended when her whole body began to shudder violently and I became concerned that something was the matter. I asked if she was okay and if I could drive her anywhere. She shook her head and began to sob quietly. One last gentle parting hug, and she slowly walked away into the night. I knew I would never see her again.

That last crazy hour with Annegret helped put things in perspective. I realized I had to go home to finish college unwed, without any kids, venereal diseases or responsibilities, and I wasn't interested in doing anything that would jeopardize those unmade and unspoken plans. The odds seemed stacked against me, and I promised myself that I would be careful.

German, English, French, American, Swedish, or anything in between, I had a tendency to imagine each girl I met as a potential soul mate, a bride, a home-maker, someone to bear my children and grow old with. I was going to be damn choosy. I wasn't going to be in a hurry, and for me to bring home a German bride she would have to be someone clearly beyond special. I didn't know how other guys looked at girls and I didn't bother to ask. But, from what I witnessed throughout our cozy little group of Amerikaners, I suspected there were others who felt the same way, and some who just wanted to see how many different pairs of bloomers they could get into.

The capture of an Ami son-in-law was the goal of many Lübecker parents, and their daughters seemed quite willing to go along with Mama and Papa. It dawned on me that I could never be sure if I was the attraction or the promise of living in America. I could sympathize with the filthy rich; dear, are you marrying me for my yacht or for me? Anyhow, I wasn't quite sure why anyone would want to leave Germany right now since it was definitely rebuilding its economy and infrastructure and creating beautiful new cities at a frantic pace.

40. The attraction

41. Unknown (blast!)

CHAPTER 11: The Wonderful World of Genetic Manipulation

Hitler's hair-brained genetic manipulations may have worked after all, for there seemed to be more pretty girls in Lübeck per square hectare than anywhere else on earth – or at least anywhere else that I had seen. This, in spite of the fact that Hitler was not welcome, and never visited Lübeck.

Although beauty is only skin deep, as they say, the skin is the first thing that one sees. I would worry about the other things later. I was certainly no stud, but after, and even during the time of Annegret, I began a trip through a progression of girls – some young women and some just outright young. And one from France and one from the good old US of A.

I found it was nice to be desired by the opposite sex, and it was impossible to focus on only one girl at a time. There were just too many, and sometimes I felt as though I was often the subject of a feminine spy network. More likely, it was just some gabby gossiping that they passed on from one to another.

It was humbling; no, I didn't know the meaning of that word. It was ego-boosting to get letters and notes from girls that I didn't even know. And yet they knew my name and address:

Anonymous letter:

Don J.,

I hope that you have reflect upon that you will improve you. I ever have thought, that you was a man who didn't like the life in the crazy Riverboat. I understand you when you will go there two or three times in the week the place which you like so much, isn't it so? But I could not understand you when you will ever go to it when you have time. You must search a hobby for you, not only the sport. But when you find all your joy in the Riverboat, than I am sorry about you. A man with so many ability like you will not find another think as going to the notorious local. No, a descent girl don't love such a fellow, who ever goes to this boat, in which are no descent girls and boys. I hope very much that you will be a short time a right man who can make a girl very happy. I who am speaking to you mean it good with you. Please belief it.

I don't know who wrote that note. Someone definitely had a thing against the Riverboat and perhaps some feelings for me. Despite the moralistic tone, I don't think it was one of the nuns from the church next door. I showed the note to several friends, and they also had no idea who the mysterious writer might be. It could even have been someone I knew – perhaps they were dating one of the guys - for they knew my name and address and the fact that I played sports and hung out a lot at the blessed Riverboat. Fräulein Anonymous never wrote again.

Dear Dan! Please be so kind and stop if you'll see me next time (only if you are alone in the car) I've got an idea!

Antje

This note was left under the windshield wiper of my VW. Sorry, Antje, I couldn't stop since I didn't know who to look for. I also wondered what her idea was; maybe she wanted to go bowling or something. This was the first and last note I got from Antje.

Sigrid E., letter:
Mon Cher Don!
Now you will see, that my handwriting is different from the letter you got some days ago. I have heard and seen some things about you, and now I know, that I am not at all the only girl in whom you took an interest. But I do not like when you are an angel in this respect. You are an Amerikaner in a strange country and you can do what you want. I will say and perhaps you should know that I have some good men friends. But everyone is nothing but a comrade for me. You are more than a comrade. I have said to you, in the Riverboat that I never would write such words in a letter, but I hope that you will not show it anyone. (Sorry, Sissi)
I said you already that you are much more for me than a comrade and I am a little sad, for you never told me that you love me. You have sometimes such indifference eyes, as if you are looking down at a flea or a cheese

I am very sorry that you go to Capri on Wednesday, and I want to write you when you are there! You are agree?? Do not forget Tuesday ½ 7. (6:30)
1000 greetings and a kiss from
Your Sissi!

Sissi was something else. I met her at the Riverboat, the one and only time she went there. It must have been on a dare, since good girls don't dance, at least not at the Riverboat. She was short, blonde, pretty, intelligent, a gifted music student, intense, and for a German girl of the times, quite independent. She would have fit right in at the head of a woman's lib march. A bonus for me, she also excelled in languages and spoke relatively fluent English and French.

Sissi was one of the good girls and spent way too much of her time trying to reform me and turn me, a small-town hick, into a cultured pearl. Stay out of the Riverboat! Let's go to the cinema, or let's go to the concert, or let's go to this fancy party so you can meet my friends or let's try this restaurant that was way to pricey for my meager soldier's pay. Or God knows what. Her intentions were good and her heart was in the right place, but I was quite content to remain the way I was.

At first, she wouldn't ride in my car with me, but insisted on meeting me at pre-determined places. She liked this one particular cinema, which I detested, since they had ushers that decided where you would sit and the movies played only in German. Worse yet, the evening started out with colored lights playing on spouting, pulsing water fountains set to organ music while everyone politely oohed and aahed, especially when the water nearly touched the ceiling, which apparently was the entire object of the exercise.

She also dragged me to several discussions and poetry readings with some of her intellectual friends on topics that I knew nothing about in a language I couldn't understand, and with people that probably wished I was someplace else. So did I. We could sit for hours and argue about basically nothing. Not really argue, but discuss various topics that I usually didn't even bother to think about. I think she was the first female to discover that I had a brain as well as a body.

Sissi was fighting a losing battle, but she was tough-minded and wouldn't give up pushing her personal agenda. I went along with it to a certain extent, but she had to make some concessions, as well. It wasn't exactly the high-class culture she had in mind, but we had some good times alone late at night on various park benches and during the few times I could convince her to get into my little VW. Here, we could sit quietly and try to find some mutually acceptable music on the cheap radio. Usually, after our date, she would run off down the street and hop on a trolley or bus and be on her way home – wherever that was. Sissi never mentioned her home or her parents and I often wondered if she was living with them. This seemed to be a big secret and it bothered me. The furtiveness of our meetings seemed unnecessary and I felt that she was afraid that her parents or someone might find out she was dating an American.

The short time we spent together was intense, but I think she sensed even before I did that she wasn't in my future plans so we just sort of drifted apart. It might have been a different story if I had planned to extend my time in Lübeck, for she was truly a special once in a lifetime type of girl.

Letter from Gisela R.:

Dear Don,

Surely you are surprised to get this letter. May be you are angry and thinking I am a foolish girl. Please don't do so! I only want to see you again, before you are going to the States. Please would you be so kind and tell me, where and when I can meet you. But if it is impossible to see you, please do tell it to me. Indeed, I would be sad, if we couldn't see us again, but never would I be angry: I always think and will think of you as a very nice boy. Hope to see you again and, please, try to make it possible!

Excuse me for writing this letter. Really I hate to write such a letter, but I saw no other way.

As ever,
Yours, Gisela

I met Gisela at a movie in our house on *Jürgen-Wullenwever Strasse*. Every so often, we would get a relatively recent Hollywood film that we would show on an ancient 16mm movie projector. We arranged all the chairs and couches in rows, pulled down the screen, assigned someone to sit and turn the take-up reel which didn't work by itself, and settled down for a couple hours of pure escapism.

Gisela came along with a friend that was dating one of the guys and since she was obviously alone, I invited her to sit with me during the film. It was a good choice for both of us, for we got along quite well from the start. During the film, I yawned, stretched, and accidentally put my arm up and around her shoulders and she didn't mind. I took that as a good sign. She even snuggled a little bit closer on the couch.

The movie ended and we went for a quiet walk down the path in our back yard to the *Wakenitz*. Here, we sat and talked and hugged a bit on the rickety dock that I was building; I had plans to get a kayak later, and I didn't want to have to get in it from the muddy shore. Besides, the dock would be a nice make-out place to sit and view the skyline of Lübeck, just as we were doing at that moment. Gisela was a nursing student at the hospital just a few blocks from our house. She was short, with brown hair, hazel eyes, well constructed and quite pretty. Best of all, she spoke decent English.

As the hour grew late, I asked if she wanted a ride home, but she declined as she had come with her friend and she felt she should leave with her, as well. That was okay with me; we walked back to the house and she left. That was it.

I ran into her a few times over the course of the next few weeks; usually she came to the house with a friend and sometimes she would allow me to walk her half way back to her dorm near the hospital. But that was about as far as Gisela and I went. No serious romance, no serious anything and to receive a letter from her asking to meet one more time didn't make much sense to me. I asked myself, if she was so interested, why didn't she indicate so earlier? I was puzzled and not sure of what to do. So I did nothing. There were just too many other viable options out there to worry about just one. I felt bad about not answering, but decided it was probably the correct thing to do.

42. Three Mädchen with various signals

Not everyone was entranced by our foreign presence, for I knew that many girls definitely did not want their parents to know they were hanging around Americans. Perhaps this was due to latent WWII feelings, for we, particularly the English, did bomb Lübeck quite thoroughly and played hell with their old churches and cathedrals. Or maybe it was our undeserved reputation as hell-raisers and no-gooders. In any case, there was a never-ending supply of young *mädchen* to go around and around and around. It was almost like a whirlwind. The problem was, there were so very, very, many who were truly special.

None more special than Chris, who, if we had been a frat house, would have been the Sweetheart of Sigma Chi. Hands down. She was sweet, pretty, fun, intelligent and very much attached to Chick Rogers. Everybody hated him. (And they broke up sometime after I left Lübeck.)

43. Chris – who was already spoken for

44. See?

CHAPTER 12: Crossing the Channel

Someone gave me a note from some chick, Emma something or other, in London that was seeking a pen pal. Ya, right. You're seeking a way to get the hell out of England. Anyway, we wrote back and forth a few times and on the spur of the moment, I decided to take one of my breaks in London. Not necessarily to see her, but to see what London looked like. I decided to go alone but at the last minute, a DF'r, Dick Strader, decided to go along. We bravely hopped a train at the Lübeck *Hauptbahnhof* and were on our way. We chugged through Hamburg, a really flat part of Germany, then into Holland, which was even flatter, past a bunch of windmills and finally ended up in the Hook of Holland, where a ferry to Harwich, England awaited.

We watched in awe as the ferry managed to swallow the entire train into its gaping yaw. For the crossing, we had to get out of the train cars and work our way up several decks to a cafeteria where we ate dinner. Eventually, we found our way to a barracks-type cabin equipped with bunk beds. Time to sleep and awaken in jolly old England.

Unfortunately, Mother Nature had other thoughts. The weather was frightful, with vicious winds, cold, and a spiteful rain. The ferry was scheduled to leave in the early evening, but the sea was too wild for safety, so we had to spend the afternoon patiently waiting. Someone finally deemed it fit for travel, so the ferry departed just before dark. What a ride! Whoever the nitwit was that OK'd the crossing should have been shot. The waves were so high that the fishing boats that were stupid enough to be out would entirely disappear in the troughs, only to bob back up about forty feet in the air. These people were nuts.

I finally decided there wasn't much I could do except hope the captain knew what he was doing while I tried to get some sleep, as I had been up for over 24 hours. I crawled, fully clothed, into the bottom half of a bunk bed that was provided for us weary travelers and promptly found myself bounced off the floor (the deck) several times before I finally fell into a sleep of exhaustion.

The next morning I stepped outside to the railing. A perfect sunrise glinted off an absolutely surreal flat and waveless sea. We were sailing through glass into Harwich and London was only a few train hours away.

After arriving at Liverpool station in London, we followed the directions to a B&B that someone had given to Dick and moved the little bit of luggage we had to a tiny room three flights upstairs. We had to promise to meet the landlady's strict condition that we absolutely, unequivocally, would not bring girls "home" to have an orgy. Promise given, we hopped into a taxi for central London and set out to explore the city. We walked and walked for what seemed like days, exploring as many sights as we could cram into haphazard wanderings. Buckingham Palace; Parliament; Westminster Abbey; Trafalgar Square; Tower of London; Piccadilly; Wimpy's. Exhausted, we taxied back to our B&B and fell into bed.

I awoke late and leaving Dick to his own doings, followed instructions from our trusty landlady, and ventured into the underground Tube. It wasn't all that difficult and I ended up back on Trafalgar Square where I was to meet Emma. I sat by a huge sculptured Lion. I waited along with a bevy of perpetually hungry pigeons and sure enough, along came a dowdy, plain, pleasant looking girl with frizzy hair. Don? I gulped.

We decided to take in a movie, which was a treat in itself, and we sat there without much to say, with her hand high up on my leg. After the movie, I politely took her to her bus stop and rapidly retreated to the safety of the B&B. Sorry, Emma, but we just weren't a match. The day was pretty much wasted.

45. Double-decker bus stop

The next day Dick and I broadened our knowledge of England on a tour boat ride up the Thames where we putted past the mighty Royal Yacht "Britannica" to the highlight of the tour - the exact spot where the Pirate Blackbeard was strapped to the pilings to be drowned by the rising tide.

Back on dry land, the creepiness extended into a dead run through Madame Toussard's wax museum. What a scary place. Worse than any graveyard. We heard that no one had ever managed to stay an entire night there without going insane and since you had to be a little bit nuts to try it, I could understand why. It was bad enough in the daylight.

As Dick was from somewhere out East, and therefore much more sophisticated than I, we once again wandered over to the theater district, past the Astoria with Michel Todd's "Around the World in 80 Days" and "The Judy Garland Show" at the Dominion Theater, and "The Flesh is Weak "at the Cameo Royal. The huge billboard above the entrance caused me to stop for a Kodak moment; it proclaimed in bold letters, "The Shame of London Exposed! Come in and then go Home and Warn your Daughters!"

46. Typical London scene

Since we didn't have any daughters, we kept on walking to Her Majesty's Theatre and the fabulous stage-play, "No Time For Sergeants" starring Andy Griffith. Dick had purchased tickets earlier. I knew nothing about the play, but the title was right and worth the price of admission, alone. Except for the Rockettes in Rockefeller Center, which didn't count, I had never seen a real professional stage play before and I was ready to be entranced. I was. We sat high up in the opera seats split several guts for most of the evening, especially at the ludicrous Mr. Griffith making all the toilet seats in the latrine stand at attention as the sarge walked in. Truly classy hilarity, that's for sure.

What a never-to-be-forgotten night that was, especially following the truly forgettable moments of the previous afternoon. After a hefty late night snack we both found that our pocketbooks were running on empty, so we decided to go back a few days earlier than planned. After one last morning of London on the cheap, we caught the train for the continent, planning to be bored again for a long night's passage across the channel. Fate must have been trying to make amends, for soon after leaving the port, a really nice looking girl caught my eye.

And I think I caught hers. It wasn't long before we were chatting and she turned out to be the first Finnish girl I had ever met. She spoke presentable English, but after a short while, we were doing more than talking. Her name was Kylliki Kyttala from Helsinki and we spent most of the evening seriously making out in various parts of the ship

As the clock zipped past midnight, however, her little brother found us and told her it was time for her to return to their cabin. Before we parted, we swapped embarkation cards with all pertinent info, including passport number, address and the fact that she was a student born exactly one year after me. Strange.

Our handwriting was barely legible due to the extreme vibration of the ferry and not because of the vibrating we had done earlier. The next morning as we disembarked at the Hook of Holland, I looked for her, but never saw her again. Ever. But now I knew first hand why some of the guys headed up north to the Scandinavian cities every chance they had.

47. The card

CHAPTER 13: Back to my lovely home

The rest of the trip back to Camelot was uneventful. However, shortly after my return I received what was to be, quite possibly, my greatest physical thrill while in Lübeck. I had bought a shiny new pocket knife in London, made by the Wilkinson sword people. I also bought a small portable *Gründig* radio for my room. Unfortunately, the plug wouldn't fit into the extension cord that I had plugged in the 220 volt wall socket. So I trotted around the corner to a nearby electrical supply shop and bought the correct plug for the extension cord. After supper, I went back to my room, sat down on the bunk, grabbed my knife, and proceeded to cut the plug off the cord. Unfortunately, I had forgotten to unplug the cord!

A blinding spark shot halfway across the bedroom and whole house was plunged into darkness as a powerful tingling sharpness traveled nearly to my armpit. I looked down in the gloom, shaking my hand, and saw that my fancy new knife had been burned halfway through the smoking and glowing blade. Luckily, no one was around to witness my stupidity; luckily, too my Wilkinson blade was sharp enough to cut through the wire with one quick stroke. Or else I would have been pretty well fried. Most likely, well done.

48. View from St. Peter's *(Petrikirche)* wobbly spire

It was nice to get back to JW *Strasse* and spend some time exploring this city that I called home. Lübeck has an ancient history, going back about 800 years, give a take a century. It flourished for hundreds of years as one of the leaders of the *Hanseatic* League, which was a trade organization built around the buying and selling of salt. Much of the area containing the old salt warehouses around the canal harbors had gotten leveled on March 29, 1942. Many of the nearby churches were damaged in the process and most of them still needed work on their spires. Along the harbors, the rubble had been cleared away, but many of the ancient buildings were still empty shells.

I heard there were submarine pens there or at least submarine repair facilities, but I couldn't verify it. Nobody wanted to talk much about the war. Especially to Americans. In fact, I often had trouble convincing people that I was an American, since there were so few of us around and Lübeck was technically in the British zone.

Anyway, the town still had a medieval air, with its brick buildings, tall pointy facades and cobblestone streets, better known as ankle-twisters and it was a fun place to just amble around, looking. The harbor area, including the infamous street of prostitution, *Clemenstrasse,* was not a particularly friendly place to visit at night. There were tales of deadly bar fights between visiting crews from various eastern block countries and once in a while, it was told, somebody could get drugged and wake up shanghaied as a crew member far out at sea. I couldn't verify that either, but it was enough to keep me at bay.

One of the guys, Brownie, told me he was in a waterfront dive one night, trying to act the tough guy and as he leaned on the bar, talking to the guy next to him he said, *"Ich bin ein gangster aus Chicago."* The guy looked at him, reached under his jacket and whipped out a huge 45 Colt revolver, plunked it on the bar and said, *"Ich bin ein gangster auch!"* (also) Brownie left shortly thereafter and never returned. In fact, he eventually became the only guy I knew that got kicked clean out of Lübeck. (As told by Mort Weston.)

49. *Marienkirche* from *Petrikirche*

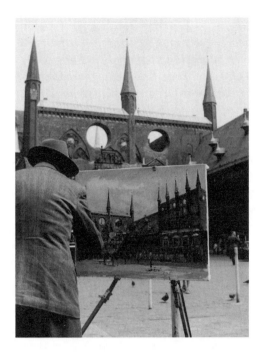

50. The ever-present *Kohlmarkt* painter

51. *Kohlmarkt,* from *St. Petri*; photo by GB Harry Walthall

Jack Weber:

Our frequent travels took some of us north to Scandinavia. From the mother of all Hauptbahnhofs in Lübeck. By land or der schnell zug to Grossenbrode Kai on the German north coast, followed by a rough seas ferry boat ride (train and all) to Gedser, Denmark, then on to the capital of the land of the smoked herring. That destination was the wonderful city of Copenhagen. Oh my God, the Danes! What a discovery. What a race of people. They knew how to party, eat well, drink with abandon and the lady Danes were a real treat. On my first trip, I met a Danish Jew by the name of Meno Fahrholt and stayed at his family's hotel. He was one of the few living Danish Jews that our old Nazi buddy, Adolf, didn't eliminate during WWII.

However, my most treasured find in Copenhagen was one extraordinary Danish lass by the name of Kirsten Kraunsoe. We met in the world-famous Tivoli Gardens at an outdoor band concert. She was a multilingual guide for the tourist board of the city of Copenhagen. On that day, Kirsten was in charge of a group of elderly folks from Spain. I followed along with the tour all afternoon. Caramba! The real "fandango" was to follow later when we met at the all-Danish club, Tropicana. Needless to say, she possessed many talents for a young eighteen year-old Nordic beauty. Yumpin-Yimminy. Vive le spontaneous combustion. My newly found friend was a beautiful, intelligent and interesting young woman and as a bonus, let it be known that she definitely was standing in front of the line when they handed out tits. Fantastico. Copenhagen. My true street of dreams. Skol!

Jon Hunter:

Then there was the summer on Fehrmarn Island and the two incidences I recall was the truck wreck when two geese ran out in front of us and we ended up in a muddy ditch. However, the best was when Roy Clark, the only Black in our detachment, took off his clothes and went down to the nudist colony – who else was with us? – I remember we stopped to talk to one family and asked how do you join and they looked at us and said it looks like you just did. Of course, Roy was a big curiosity since I am sure most of the nudists had never seen many Blacks, much less a naked one.

CHAPTER 14: Way Beyond Special

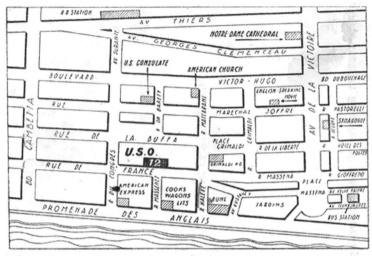

52. Map of Nice central city

53. Me on the east Nice overlook

To Nancy from Nice; *Je départ mais mon coeur rester a vous.*

Nancy from Nice was absolutely one of the most beautiful girls I have ever seen. Black hair, light skinned, dark green eyes, a tad over five feet tall, she was a cross between Natalie Woods and Elizabeth Taylor and better looking than both of them. I met her at the USO in Nice. I had gone there with Dick Nelson and one other guy, on one of our illicit border crossings into France courtesy of Mad Magazine. None of us spoke any French and most of the French didn't speak English.

It all started somewhere in the heart of France when I ordered off the menu and was served a platter of lamb's brains. By the time we reached the Riviera, we were tired of not knowing what we were eating. After we checked into a cheap hotel near the train station in Monaco, we decided a drive down to the USO in Nice for some real American food seemed like a good idea. After some chasing around to find the place, the cafeteria was closed but it was still possible to get a couple left-over hot dogs. What luck. But it wasn't totally bad as we found out they were having a "meet the locals" dance that evening.

And there she was, standing shyly at the side of the dance floor with a couple of her friends, and my eyes, heart, kidneys and everything else dropped right down through my shoes. Breathing deeply to settle myself, I managed to get up enough nerve to ask her to dance. She accepted. This was it. I was hooked for life. Mother, here I come. I think she felt the same; from this point on, she refused to dance with anyone else.

When the music finally stopped and the evening ended at some ungodly early hour, we could hardly let each other go. But we had no choice; we had to leave. I managed to cram all of us into the car and drove off to deposit the girls somewhere near their homes as it would be unseemly to drop them off on their front doorstep. Using sign language and scribbling on a piece of paper, Nancy and I agreed to meet again next evening in front of the USO. I was ecstatic.

The night was young and I was beautiful. So back to our chintzy hotel in Monaco we went. The Monte Carlo Casino wasn't that far away from our room so off we went to see what it was like. After a quick walk around the building, including the steps and gardens facing the Mediterranean, I ended up being the only one that wanted to go in. The others went off to drink beer but I was feeling lucky.

54. Ticket to the Casino

55. Nellie at Monte Carlo casino

Despite the casino in *Travemünde*, I didn't know anything about big-time gambling. I walked around checking out the various tables and being checked out by a wrinkly-faced old hag in a thread-bare evening gown. I didn't want any part of that decided it wasn't too smart to nod and say "*bon soir*" to anyone over 70. After watching for about half an hour, I knew I was too unsure of myself to get involved in any of the card games. Besides, they were playing them all in French. I settled on roulette, as it was just basically red and black colors and numbers. I bought about five dollars worth of 200-franc chips, about 50 cents each, and sat down and watched.

It didn't take too long to figure it out, so I tried guessing individual numbers since that seemed to be the way to get rich quick. But after I lost a few times by playing the wrong numbers, I realized that trying to figure out where that little white ball would stop was damn near impossible. However people kept trying and despite the fantastic pay-off if you accidentally did hit the right number, I saw very few people winning anything. The odds were really high, like 20 to 1 or even more for some combinations, but the odds of my money running out were even greater. There was another way to play that seemed to make more sense to me. It was definitely simple and had a 50-50 chance of winning on every turn. The odds weren't good – only one to one, but if I bet two chips and I won, I would get two chips from the croupier. I could understand that. With this system, I played only the colors, red or black. Nothing else.

After the croupier spun the ball in the wheel and as he called "*en le pleu*" - it sounded like "end the play" - I sensed that the ball would stop in red, for instance, so I quickly put my chips on the red square and waited to collect my winnings.

And win I did. And again and again. It was so unfair. Either that little ball was telling me something or my senses were so in tune with the ball and wheel that I KNEW what that color would be. I would almost have bet my life on it. After I had collected several stacks of chips, I began to get bolder and place even more and more of them on the squares until I had this huge wall of chips. People were starting to gather around to watch and I just kept on winning.

Nothing lasts forever. Just as quickly as it appeared, my Midas touch disappeared and I finally lost. It hurt. I tentatively placed one lonely chip out as a test and I lost again. It was time to pack it in. I got a basket, shoveled my chips in it and headed for the cashier. Giddy, I didn't pay any attention to how much I had won, but it seemed like at least a medium-sized fortune. At least for me. If I had been playing with 10,000 franc chips, I could have bought a yacht. I could have bought Monaco. But, for now, that wasn't my interest. That lay some miles away in Nice. I wondered if she was thinking of me; Nancy and a fortune. This was indeed my lucky night.

The next day passed slowly, and I spent a good portion of it trying to memorize French phrases from a Berlitz handbook. But there was definitely too much "la plume de ma tante," in it, and I wasn't interested in talking about my aunt's pen with Nancy. She spoke absolutely no English, and I spoke about five words in French. The famous question, *"voulez vous coucher avec mois?"* and I didn't think these were appropriate with this girl. At least not for quite some time.

I dumped my friends somewhere near the rocky beach in Nice, then drove the few blocks to the USO where I swallowed some food and waited outside for her to arrive. It seemed like several hours passed, but arrive she did, and I could breathe comfortably again. Somehow we decided it would be nice to take a drive - to drive anywhere – since being together was the most important thing. Like a horse returning to the barn, I headed back to Monaco on the now-familiar route along the windy road high above the Mediterranean.

Driving and reading a phrase book doesn't work, so we sat in silence, holding hands whenever possible and listening to radio music from the tinny-sounding speakers. It was a marvelous ride.

I parked my tan VW directly in the street in front of the Casino and we walked around to the promenade behind the building. Here, the view was spectacular as the moon was rising over the sea and up into a perfectly clear dark blue sky. There was a soft light from the Casino windows and a few globe-shaped light posts, but the area was basically dark. That was nice and convenient if you didn't want to be seem, but it was impossible to communicate via phrase book. So spoken words were out and all we had left was the universal language.

We hugged, kissed, and basically held onto each other for what seemed only a few minutes but in actuality was probably a hour or so. Then it was time to return to a lighted area and try to say something courtesy of Mr. Berlitz. He did a lousy job, but we both took it in good humor and happily headed back to the car for the drive back to Nice. Saddest drive of my young life, for I knew I had to leave for Lübeck the next day. Even the promise of returning to Camelot paled in contrast to being with this girl - language difficulties or not. If God made Man to be with Woman, then this was the perfect match. Damn the tower of Babel, anyway.

The night was still young, maybe ten o'clock or so and I parked a few doors from her house. We carefully exchanged addresses and as best we could, solemnly pledged to seriously study each other's language. I promised to return in a month or two - as soon as possible - and a last long lingering kiss and tearful *au revoir* and she dashed off into her house. I was thoroughly smitten - more so than any other time in my young life. I sobbed to myself all the way back to Monaco.

56. My last words to Nancy from Nice; I go, but my heart stays with you. I really meant it this time.

But what the hell; I recovered fast. I still had my mini-fortune and a couple hours left in the day. I blitzed back to Monte Carlo for I knew the Casino was still open. I walked in, exchanged my wad of francs for chips and promptly proceeded to lose every dime of it. It was obviously a portent of things to come, for after one exchange of letters with Nancy from Nice, I never heard from her again. Maybe I insulted her or something, trying to write a letter in French with a dictionary, God knows what I said. I know what I intended, but it probably came out ass backward or something. I stashed away a scribbled note from Nancy and one lonely green plastic 200 franc chip from those fantastic heart-breaking nights on the Riviera. For at least two special, wonderful nights, I had the girl that was way beyond special and she was mine, all mine.

57. Monaco harbor

CHAPTER 15: The Russians Are Coming!

Back at the home front in Lübeck, a couple of episodes reminded us that, yes, we were in the Army, and yes, we were also in a Cold War. The first incident happened one mid shift, the long one from midnight to eight a.m., when everything and everybody was a little sleepy as not much was usually happening, radio-wise. Once in a while, as we were putzing around the lower frequencies, and the radio signals were bouncing just right from weather system to system, it was possible to pull in a commercial station from the U.S. But that was the limit to our excitement.

Around two a.m. one of these sleepy shifts, with Wes Roach and Marion Weston more or less on duty, a German guy burst through the flimsy door of our quonset hut. The door opened sharply inward against Wes and jarred him quickly out of his stupor and he reacted like the trained ASA killer that he was by tossing off his ear phones and pushing with all his might to close the door. The German flew out the door and landed on his butt on the ground. Wes jumped up and grabbed a carbine that we kept above the door – just for cases like this and shooting an occasional crow – and he and Mort held the intruder at bay. The man started babbling nonsense in German and started to come slowly at Wes. Wes quickly chambered a round and fired a shot just over the German's head. That apparently got the Deutcher's attention for he fell to the ground, blubbering and peeing in his pants.

The gunshot rousted the troops in the crypto hut and as their work was somewhat more sensitive than ours, they had an established procedure that would bring the German gendarmes post-haste. They arrived in a short ten minutes and took the culprit into custody to what fate no one of us knows.

When the rest of us heard the story, we had some serious questions that never got answered. Was this just some dumb-shit drunk out on a dare? If so, he surely wouldn't go out to a darkened site alone at two in the morning. How did he get out there? Others had to be involved. Where were they? Who were they? Would a real spy do something as stupid as this?

We could understand the curiosity angle as the good citizens of Lübeck were infinitely interested in what we were doing out there. They were always asking questions, but we were under strict orders not to discuss our work with anybody, anytime. The Russian language translators couldn't even let anyone know they spoke Russian. If you screwed up in the ASA, there was always the very real threat of being sent to the infantry, losing your secret clearance, or in the worse cases, being court-martialed and sent to Leavenworth. And the absolutely worst case, of course, would be to be sent away from Lübeck Anywhere else was definitely a downer.

What did this guy hope to prove by just bursting into a hut? Just to see the equipment so he could tell his drinking buddies? That seemed more like something WE would do. If he truly was a spy, then he probably saw enough in those few seconds to verify any questions he may have had. After all, it wouldn't take a genius to guess that soldiers in a secret site with a tall, skinny radio tower right on the East/West German border just might be listening in on the Russian's Big Red Machine who were within stone-throwing distance in *Schwerin*. But then, the average citizen didn't and still doesn't know about such things.

So, for a while we were on sort of heightened alert, which meant checking the gate once in a while – I guess the guy just climbed over it – and bracing a chair up against the door. To be honest, we were all a little nervous for a few days since there really wasn't much else we could do; if someone wanted to get in the site, they would get in. It wasn't that difficult, as Herr Blubberhead proved. Of course, no one bothered to tell any of us what the real story was. I didn't really lose any sleep over it.

Another Cold War incident that could have proven more serious involved a carload of Russian officers. Because the Allies were limited to only one highway to get into Berlin, of course we had to do something to prove our equally base human nature. So, by decree of the Allied Commanders, the Soviet ambassador corps, including all their military attaches and plain everyday spies were allowed to drive only on certain designated highways throughout Germany. Now, with the huge and wide-spread road system in Germany, that would prove to be an unenforceable rule. About the only way to insure that the

Russians were staying on the correct roads would be to monitor, somehow, every car, truck, motorcycle, bicycle, and pair of roller skates that they owned. I don't think we were up to that; it would have been a colossal waste of manpower and money. Anyway, the rules were there and since we had to follow theirs, I guess it was only right that they follow ours.

One bright sunshiny day a huge Mercedes limo with embassy license plates and sporting a little Russian flag on the front fender pulled up on the shoulder of the narrow country road just outside our site. They were only a couple hundred yards from Mutti's so maybe we should have invited them over for a *bier und schnitzel.*

Not really. This car was definitely on the wrong road.

Fortunately, this happened during a trick change, and some of the 058 boys were arriving for work and drove right past the Mercedes and saw the Russians taking pictures. They rushed to the compound and drove back with a few carbines and more guys from the crypto hut, which included two Russian language specialists. The Russians were quickly made to feel unwelcome as they were promptly surrounded by a group of trained and unfriendly ASA killers not knowing whether to shoot or salute. After a few minutes of shuffling around and jeez, what do we do now looks, a sort of question and answer period began, with English and bad German as the means of communication.

What are you doing here?

What are **you** doing here?

Nothing. What are you doing?

Nothing. What are **you** doing?

It was soon obvious that both sides weren't really trained as interrogators. It was quite a sight, as neither group knew exactly what to do. Here was a Russian general, a couple lower level officers, probably majors or the equivalent and a driver all dressed up in their spiffy uniforms with big round hats faced off with a circle of rag-tag U.S. soldiers dressed in white t-shirts and baggy fatigues. And carrying loaded rifles.

To top it off, two of our guys could understand every word the Russians said to each other and apparently they were more scared than we were. Their story was that they were on the way from Frankfurt to Hamburg and made the wrong turn somewhere. Not a very good story as in order to get to our site, they had to drive through Hamburg, then go the 40 odd miles to Lübeck and then circle back to *Blankensee* on narrow back roads. So they were lying. At least they could have said they were driving to Kiel or *Travemünde* which would have been somewhat more believable.

Finally, it was suggested that we escort the Mercedes back to Lübeck and let the German police handle it from there. The car was an official embassy vehicle, so the Russians knew they were immune from any prosecution. That was agreeable, so off the caravan went; one spiffy smooth black Mercedes limousine and several khaki-colored U.S. Army-issue junk-yard special three-quarter ton trucks hic-cupping down the road.

We all waited for the German police by an outdoor café at the round-about at the edge of Lübeck, and, of course, guys being guys no matter the uniform, there were eventually beers all around and the no-hard-feelings type of thing. Our guys who spoke Russian said our new friends gave no indication they were actually looking for our site and maybe they really were lost. Perhaps they were just good actors. It was more likely they were just good liars.

Our story was that we were a canteen-repair unit, but frankly that was pretty weak and an obvious bald-faced lie. A canteen repair shop, if such a thing existed, certainly wouldn't require a 100 foot radio tower. So we were liars, too. What else could we say? I can see the Russians saying to each other, "do these clowns think we're stupid?"

The end result was that now there was one high-ranking Russian officer who could personally confirm that yes indeed, it was highly likely the Americans had a listening post right on the border across from *Schwerin*. He could also make damn sure that in case anything happened, we would be the first to go.

Once again no one really knows what happened from that point on. The Police probably confiscated a couple cameras and film and let the Russkis go on their way to Hamburg or wherever. We all went back to work with one more war story for the record.

The Russians would have been amazed to know the extent of American radio surveillance along the East-West German border. It's likely that every Russian division had a detachment of ASA'ers like ours just inside the West German border, monitoring every little dah-di-dah and conversation they made by radio. Or by telephone, as the ASA was responsible for tunneling under the Berlin wall and tapping into the phone lines of the East German and Russian forces.

A U.S. Air Force hut truck even used our compound for a few weeks to monitor the rockets the Russians were launching from *Peenemünde*, on the Baltic coast. Each type of rocket gives off different identifiable sounds which would be definitely useful to know in case they had any aimed our way so we would have at least a few moments to duck for cover. This would be comparable to the U.S. Navy's listening devices planted in the various oceans of the world that can identify almost every type of whale or submarine that happens to be cruising by.

All this surveillance stuff was a huge and complex operation, and as I began to understand our mission a little better, I was amazed at just how huge and complex it really was.

Our little detachment was complete with Russian and Polish linguists, cryptographers, (cryptologists rhymes with proctologists), DF'er (direction-finders) repairmen, the whole works. We were kept pretty much compartmentalized, neither segment overlapping or involved with the other. It was the whole need to know thing.

When we heard any voice transmissions in the clear, in other words voices actually talking to each other and not in Morse code, we immediately had to notify the language guys so they could produce instant interpretation. Of course, since we were listening to the Russian tank divisions, we were all dreading the moment they would hear, "Ok, guys, lets mount up and head west to kick the shit out of those American imperialistic lying dogs – especially those little bastards in Lübeck."

Fortunately for us, most of the conversations were limited to standard Army talk, such as, "where the hell are those fuel trucks?" "What was that crap we had for breakfast, anyway?" "Who was the dog you were with last night, Boris?" And the Russian equivalent of, "yo mama!"

58. Russia Hut; courtesy of GB Harry Walthall

Note from Goodback Harry Walthall:
Christmas eve, '57 or '58 I was totally shocked to transcribe the following voice radio message in the open: "The 204th Guards Motorized Rifle Division wishes the men of the 319th ASA Company a Merry Christmas."

Another note from Harry:
When Jim Shaw and Heinke got married the Lübecker Nachrichten (newspaper) printed the following headline, in German, of course, "Local Girl Marries US Army Canteen/Mess Kit Repairman." No lie! It seems our propaganda only worked for the West Germans.

I assumed that the Russians were doing something similar to us. At least we knew for certain that some sort of spying by the Russians or East Germans was taking place on a regular basis. How could we be sure that a whore on *Clemenstrasse* or a girl we innocently met at the Riverboat or *Travemünde* wasn't working for the other side? It probably happened, but in our naiveté, we just didn't realize it. Since we were doing it at the electronic level, turn about has to be fair play.

In fact, it turns out the East Germans had a huge HUMINT network established throughout West Germany. Several thousand spies had been recruited and had infiltrated much of West Germany and the East German army had established a SIGINT force which ran up and down the border – just like our very own Army Security Agency. They were monitoring NATO military communications, and searching for early indications of a sneak NATO attack. Spying, on both sides of the border was big business. The fledgling East German spy apparatus eventually grew to become one of the legendary success stories of the Eastern Bloc, technologically rivaling that of our own NSA.

Donald Boucher:
I also recall one other incident when we were told that 2 East German spies had been apprehended around our site in Blankensee. Supposedly, they had pictures of us entering and exiting our trailers and the 2 houses in Lübeck. From what we were told, they had info on all of us including, date and place of birth, schools attended, names of family members, etc We were told that they were sentenced to 25 years in jail.....

However, I think the East Germans had severe growing pains. Around ten one foggy night that was just made for a spy movie, I was taking a girl home and noticed a man standing under a street light where *Jürgen-Wullenwever Strasse* runs into a little city park, just past our house. He had his hands tucked into a long gray trenchcoat, a fedora pulled down over his eyes and was standing very still on an empty street. The fog occasionally gets heavy in Camelot, and all that was visible on the whole street was this one person under the glow of a single streetlight. I thought this was really strange.

About an hour later, as I was returning home, the man was still standing there, and I could see the red glow of a cigarette.

When I got into the house, I was a little concerned; Lt. Bell was still there and I told him about what I had seen. He told me that it was okay; the man was an undercover German policeman on a stakeout. There had been reports of an East German spy in the neighborhood.

I wondered how much more obvious a cop could be. At least if he was trying to be sneaky, he would hide in the bushes or something. Any self-respecting spy would make a wide detour around this guy. I went to bed with an uneasy feeling about our personal security.

The next afternoon I saw Lt. Bell in the office again, and asked him about the stakeout. He told me that they caught the spy a little after midnight and I had missed all the excitement. That's all he said. Jeez, I wondered, how dumb can these spies be? If I was from the Eastern Bloc, I would definitely have some security problems to be worried about. Later I found out from some of the guys who were more involved with these things, that there actually was a foot-chase around some of the yards and through the little park before the spy was caught. But once again, no one was told what happened to him.

Donald Boucher:

In October of '56, Tom Kielty, one of our NCO's (along with Pete Heatherington and Roy Dean) and I were on the graveyard shift and were scanning the airways when we picked up traffic around 2 a.m. that the Russians were moving into Budapest, Hungary, at 6 a.m. To make a long story short, the traffic we picked up was translated, analysed, and sent to Washington through channels. We notified Lt. Patterson. The troops rushed Lübeck to the site at Blankensee and we awaited orders.

We were told the President had been given the intelligence that we intercepted. As I recall, around 4 a.m. we were told to get ready to abandon the site and head for Bremerhaven, which was our escape route. We got ready to destroy documents and equipment, if necessary. Then a second order came through that we were to stay put – that under no circumstance were we to roam around Lübeck in civilian clothes and that we needed to remember only three things – name, rank, and serial number.

The alert status under which we were operating lasted about two or three weeks. I remember VIVIDLY, however, that the next day the Lübecker Nachrichten (newspaper) carried a small blurb on an inside page requesting that the Americans conduct their maneuvers during the day so as not to awaken the citizenry in the middle of the night with their noisy vehicles.

Mike Raphael: Whoa! Mike, did you say explosive charges? Nobody told me about them – at least until now.

I can't respond to the strike, presuming there really was one, but can say, briefly, the following: We knew where the triggers were for blowing up the huts and equipment, and were on the verge of doing that one day. We had one weapon, with ammo (grease gun, in my hut, two clips), and the rest of the weapons (M1s and M1 carbines) were in the basement at the Zwingli house (and, to the best of my knowledge, no ammo). If the houses contained explosive charges and were thus wired, we didn't know that.

We also knew, as far as we could tell, that we would be overwhelmed in minutes, that the U. S. could, perhaps, hold out for 24 hours before the Russians and East Germans took Germany (all zones).

When I went to Lübeck, the lieutenant called us outside for the only and only formation we ever had, and described our battle orders, in the event we were invaded. He told us that he would take Ralph, Jerry and me with him in his Caddie and that the rest were to head toward Paris as fast as they could go. Then, "dismissed." No other discussion.

We were very aware of what was happening in Hungary months before the revolt, and some of us kept track of what happened long after we went home

Dennis Whelan:

I was a Russian Voice Interceptor in Lübeck from 2/56 to 12/56, then was reassigned to Heidelberg after losing crypto clearance due to my engagement to Margot, a Lübeck girl. There was one instance of a semblance of a strike that occurred on my watch when traffic went down because our new CO, Lt. Patterson, was going to shape us up into a "real" military outfit – inspections in full military gear were going to be enforced. We needed to be made to remember that we indeed a part of the military and not a country club

The dress of the day at that time was, to say the very least, casual – Hawaiian shirts, fatigue pants, penny loafers, safari hats – I'm sure you get the picture. In a way, we felt kind of bad for the Lt., but Lübeck was supposed to be different and he had not yet realized that. Anyway, the "slowdown" lasted about a week, as I recall.

A team of officers were sent from Rothwesten to investigate why the troops were unhappy, since traffic had drastically decreased. They investigated, had their pow-wow with the Lt. and everything returned to normal. New Hawaiian shirts suddenly appeared and replaced the old ones. Penny loafers were shined like never before and amazingly, the Russians started conversing like never before.

Don Boucher recalls the same incident:

Lt. Patterson was indeed an ROTC grad of S. Miss. U. He was still there when I left in Dec. of '56. At that time, the U. had the reputation of accepting any student that was rejected anywhere else in the US. We were not too impressed with his credentials. When he first arrived, I recall that he was intent on making the unit into a "militarily disciplined" one. Remember the Hawaiian shirts, penny loafers, fatigue pants? Not SOP dress.....I remember the very first inspection that he conducted in Blankensee....Cooper said that inspections were quite foreign to the detachment....and could the Lt. please step aside so he could take a picture of the event.....Guys were rolling on the ground with laughter. The Lt. did get his way....We shaped-up and resented it......That's when our mini "strike" took place. Traffic slowed down....Inspectors came up from Rothwesten.

I remember some of the guys "misappropriating" his jeep and stashing it in some garage on Clemenstrasse.....I remember Pete and Roy having a chat with the Lt. and educating him in the life in Lübeck. Fact: the best and most traffic came from Lübeck. Therefore, it was important to keep the troops happy...Therefore, he should drop the dress code and ask for a search party to find the jeep that his salary was now accountable for. After this fireside chat and a few "discussions" with the brass from Hq., life became a lot more relaxed and mysteriously the jeep reappeared a few days later.....And life in Lübeck resumed normalcy; newer Hawaiian shirts, polished loafers, and neatly pressed fatigue pants...

Myron Havis; an example of Commie chasing:

I was working for Wally Sundquist in operations and from time to time we would get a list of known communists in the Lübeck area from battalion. One month I noticed a name on the list - Biebrach. I told Wally that the name sounded familiar to me and if I thought about it for a while maybe I could put it together. As luck would have it, it did come to me and I told Wally, I think they're Babyface's parents. Babyface was Herma Biebrach and she had gone out with a lot of guys. I was even invited to dinner at her house with her parents. And now they were marked down as known communists, uh oh! What made it worse, was that one of the newer guys had fallen for her and apparently gotten engaged to her. Now, things heated up.

Wally had to report it because of the engagement and the next thing you know we're descended on by a group of plainclothes CIC agents. The first step in their investigation was to assemble the entire company in our movie room over the dining room, hand out a questionnaire asking everyone to list all sorts of things about any acquaintance with one Herma Biebrach and also to list all German females where social contact was involved. As I recall, Al Goldfine listed all first names and when they called him on this he replied, "Who asks last names?"

The group was narrowed down to a very few. Unfortunately, I was one of only two who knew her well and had also met her parents and I had to undergo some very unpleasant interrogation in the basement at Blankensee.

There was nothing there, so it all dissipated, but those were very tense days. We even had a supposed chaplain from, I think, Corps HQ. In retrospect, I would guess he was just another CIC agent put in our midst to see if he could ferret out any info surreptitiously. Many months after, when everything had blown over, I ran into Babyface and she told me that the CIC had taken her to Frankfurt and given her a polygraph test. They questioned her about Sgt. Havis, she told me but this name didn't ring a bell with her, because just like Al Goldfine, she only knew first names - I was only Myron to her.

Sort of general knowledge:

One late night, a particularly despised CO, nicknamed The Bear, (his real name was Russian for bear) trying to sneak over the compound gate in order to catch the guys snoozing, ruined all his attire on the barbed wire when a faithful comm center worker, who shall remain unnamed, sprayed a .30 caliber burst over his head. The scared-shitless upside-down Captain had to be rescued and untangled from the barbed wire.

Special note by Dennis Whelan: (Over four decades later; now working in Russia and the United States. My, how things change with time.)

But by a really wild coincidence, one of my best friends here in Russia served in a signals unit that listened in on our troops at the same time we were across the border listening in on theirs. Actually, he's not in Russia any longer--he's a biophysicist currently living in Maryland and working on a DARPA grant on an invention of his that uses biorhopsin (I think it's called) as a kind of photomemory. How the world turns...

59. Me in the mirror with my trusty Kodak Retina IIC. Speaking of photos, this is how most of the photos in this book were taken.

CHAPTER 16: Almost a Witness to an Execution

In early spring, I made a trip by myself to Darmstadt, a town slightly to the south of Frankfurt. I had gone there at the insistence of my mother to visit "Rosie's" family. Rosie had married one of the boys from my home village who was in the Air Force version of the ASA, and she had a younger sister, Heidi, that was now of marrying age. I was sent to scout her out and vice versa. They were a nice enough family, but young, a tad bit plump, and cute Heidi was not for me.

60. Heidi with *Mutter u.Vater*

I arrived in Darmstadt the night before the occasion and having next to no money, decided to sleep in my VW. I parked near the city library, which had two huge stone lions guarding the entrance staircase, so it seemed safe enough. As I learned from my intense interlude with Annegret, the VW Beetle is not made for horizontal bliss, even with the seats tilted all the way back it takes some getting used to. After endless twisting and turning, I finally awoke around five a.m. from what constituted my sleep. It was still dark with a hint of sunrise in the sky. Just light enough to see by. The streets were empty with only a noisy delivery truck or two rattling by. I unwound out of my cramped and near-fetal position and walked creakily over to a nearby pond to take a pee and check out a couple swans that were beginning to feed. I had my camera and tried to take some pictures in the early morning dawn.

As I was eyeing the swans, a man came along - stubble beard, short cropped hair, dark leather jacket – and started to talk to me in German. I could understand some of what he was talking about, but most of it went right over my head. He was trying to get the swans to come in closer to the shore so I could get a better picture. Apparently, I was of some interest to him, I don't know why, but he was friendly enough and didn't seem to present any particular danger. I was not comfortable talking to a total stranger in a tiny park with swans way before breakfast, so my warning antennae were humming.

As he talked on and I muttered an occasional uh-huh, ja or whatever words I thought might be appropriate, it finally became apparent that he was inviting me to witness an execution. I was under the impression that capital punishment was forbidden in Germany, so I became apprehensive as I wondered just who was going to be the executee. I hoped it wouldn't be me.

He made it crystal clear as he held his index finger up to his head and made as though he were firing a gun. "Pow," he said, "*um sechs uhr*." At six o'clock, only about half an hour away. It was time for me to leave. I managed to tell him, "*nein, danke schön,*" no thanks, I had to go right now. He shrugged and with a cheery "*auf wiedersehen,*" waved goodbye as I quickly left the park for the safety of my car.

I had no idea what this was all about, but unless this guy was totally coo-coo, someone was going to die at six that morning. Obviously, not legally. As I drove off shivering from this surreal scene, I wondered if the Germans weren't doing some of this stuff under the table and if this wasn't a handy way to get rid of various spies and other undesirables that they were so efficient at killing only a decade and a half earlier. Or maybe it was a gangland killing or just a figment of this guy's imagination. I was proud that I had the sense to get the hell out of there. I didn't really want to know.

CHAPTER 15: On the Really Hardwood

Shortly after my visit to Darmstadt, I received an invitation from a Lübeck sport club, the *LBV Phönix,* to play on their basketball team. I'm not sure who all was invited, but a couple of us said, why not? We joined up. We practiced and played our games in a field house a couple blocks away. It was the coldest building I have ever been in and the floor of the basketball court was made of end-grain hardwood.

61. He shoots, he scores (He is me.)

It was like two by fours laid end-wise and glued together and was the hardest surface I have ever seen. It was tougher than concrete, and if you fell, you would get severely damaged. We also played a few games in Hamburg; the highlight of the away games was riding with the women's team in a big bumpy bus.

The games in Hamburg were ferocious, as we had bombed the living crap out of that fair city only some 15 years earlier. As a result, we Amis nearly got decapitated after each shot and spent a lot of time picking our battered bodies out of the bleachers. There was more than enough invitations to fight during and after those games, but cooler heads on the *Phönix* prevailed and we managed to escape, bloody, often beaten, but unbowed. After all, we had the bus ride with the women's team to look forward to.

The club was typical of European sports clubs, having its own athletic fields, club house, and teams in many sports from kayaking to basketball to soccer. In many respects, they were a civilian version of American colleges and universities. However, they provided teams for people of all ages. They also featured social activities such as fancy balls, regular dances, parties, and other sports-related get-togethers. Most of the girls were pretty fun and nice to kid around with and occasionally I suspected someone was messing around in the back of the bus. But no one I could get seriously interested in. Well, maybe one. That was *Gabriele*, the mis-named star player for the women's team. Short, stocky, tough as nails, hell, she was stronger and faster than I was. (But I could shoot better.) We talked a lot, so she could practice her English, but that's about all it amounted to. She was really nice and a fun person to be with and helped prove to me that beauty was not always visible on the surface.

62. Movie night. Dick Nelson – just waiting for the party to start

CHAPTER 18: Parties and Such

There always seemed to be a party of some sort going on at our house. Usually, we would start off watching a bad Hollywood movie, then move into the bar/dining area where the tables were pushed out of the way to make a dance floor and then on to various bedrooms or cars or the grass on the lawn down by the *Wakenitz*.

Often times, I was sent down to the Riverboat to recruit attendees of the feminine persuasion, and since I didn't imbibe, had more fun watching the guys slowly drink themselves into oblivion and straight into the inevitable hangover. One party in particular, introduced me personally to Danish girls. Well, one Danish girl, in particular. A sergeant who made the trip up to Copenhagen as often as possible, brought his girl friend, whom he introduced as Lisa, his fiancée, to show off to the guys. She was short, blonde, stacked, and gorgeous. Sarge was indeed a lucky guy. Lisa was the typical Danish girl as described by those who often partook of Copenhagen's feminine hospitality. She appeared to be in her mid to late 20's and somewhat older than the girls I was used to being with.

As the night wore on, the Sergeant became more and more attached to his bar stool and more and more interested in his cups. His fiancée of the moment, Lisa, became less and less interested in him and more and more interested in me. Either she asked me or I asked her, but we began to dance. She was slightly tipsy, but as we danced, practically stitched together, and got seriously into the sensuous rhythm of the music, she began to groan softly. She squeezed tighter and tighter against my body. and whispered in my ear that she was ready to do anything with me and could we get out of here to somewhere private? Like right now? I almost swooned with delight at the thought, but casting a glance at the hapless sergeant, who was finally beginning to notice his girl friend's "togetherness" with someone other than him, I decided that retreat made more sense than valor and danced her over to the bar.

At that moment, Lisa swooned, or at least pretended to swoon, and fell limply backward in my arms. I finished ungluing myself and dragged her over to the bar and left her propped up in the Sarge's not-too-stable arms. I then made haste before he realized who I was. I was in no hurry to place myself in a position to get booted out of Lübeck. No matter how enticing the reason. But I hadn't had such fun since the day I climbed up to the top of the radio tower and surveyed the lovely flat land surrounding our site.

At another party, this time one of the official German holidays, the bar was freshly stocked and the dining room, nee ball room, was crowded with most of the available Lübeckers and native locals of every stripe, including the city *Bürgermeister.* Unfortunately, several of the girls from the infamous red light street, *Clemenstrasse,* had also been invited. One of them walked over to the mayor, called him *"liebchen"* and worse yet, called him by his first name, and then gave him a big hug. This didn't go over too well with the *Bürgermeister's* wife, but somehow we managed to avoid a riot.

As a result of this happy get together with the local citizens, several of us were invited to have a nightcap at some German family's house a few blocks away. This couple was maybe in their mid-40's. After the usual handshaking and introduction during which I never did catch the name, we were asked to put our coats in the bedroom. As we walked in, we noticed the gentleman of the house's black SS uniform, complete with a red swastika arm band, hanging on the closet door. I thought those arm bands were against the law. There were also various pictures of him with other Nazi figures of World War II and a bayonet lying on a dresser. Lübeck was not noted for its Nazi background so we found this more than a bit disconcerting and decided that it would be prudent to make an exit as soon as possible. In conversation, we discovered that the former SS man, like all Germans we met, never killed or fought an American in WWII. I wondered who our guys were always being killed by and, in return, were busy killing, since it seems 99.9% of the German army was busy on the eastern front in Russia.

In any case, we managed to make our excuses and got out of there quickly and returned to the relative safety of *Jürgen-Wollenwever Strasse.*

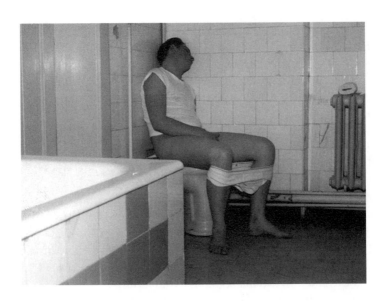

63. The morning after; not exactly France

64. The authentic & correct spelling

CHAPTER 19: Introducing Carole

April 20
Dear Don,

Have bought African cactus to promote feeling of unheard of springtime - it's April in Paris under a legendary type sun - it's black, black today - and if I say another word the spirit of reader will be the same.

It interests me to know how two tired, blurry-eyed g.i.'s conquered the German hi-ways after two hours of sleep and minus a chocolate bar - we didn't mean to keep the thing from you soldiers but thanks anyway for adding extra pleasure to a one-time, one-sided, monotonous breakfast.

Along with invitation to the Young Nation Communist Society which is held every Tuesday, I received announcement that we have Ascension holidays, or something of that sort, the 23rd of May - so, if the Army is giving out extra grants that weekend, you can come too. Okay, it's all settled! We're gonna' try the helicopter flight if it's not too expensive - rumor has it that it's better than the fair itself. Only rumor, mind you, probably the only thing which lives to tell about it.

We've found it very hard to begin our lives again as students. The farce of going to school has ceased to be funny - one of these days I fear I'm going to pay for lack of attendances at classes - it used to be fun to have lots of time and nothing to do with it, but the old question of what next is beginning to prey on idle mind. Sorry, didn't mean to use you as beast of burden for my petty problems which I'm sure carry no weight in the mind of a born athlete.

Thanks for the very nice evening Monday nite - enjoyed the walk, talk, and for the first time, the rain...I wonder what you look like in the sun? Maybe there'll be better days in Brussels... well ... hello to Irvin.. and.. any time you feel the spark of composition coming on - I'm always a good listener.

Bye for now!

Carole

CHAPTER 20: 'Twas on the Isle of Capri That I Found Her

At the beginning of April, we were several days into a ten day furlough and Irv and I spent the night sleeping in our car just outside Naples. We had just driven from Rome and were planning to drive around the Bay of Naples in order to catch the ferry from Sorrento to Capri. I don't know why I wanted to go there; I just remembered a song, "Twas on the Isle of Capri That I Found Her," and I thought it would be a neat place to see.

Three of us who happened to have time off at the same time started out from Lübeck in my little VW. It was common to go on leave with anyone who had the same leave time and was a good way to share expenses and have some traveling companionship. Dick Nelson wanted to be dropped off in Munich, and I continued on the way with my new friend, Irvin Deranger. He was newly arrived at our house at #10 and was a good looking Cajun from a small town in Louisiana at the mouth of the Mississippi River. He seemed like a really nice guy, but I didn't know much about him except that he spoke a version of French that nobody in France could understand. His English was no better as it was so heavily accented that none of us Lübeckers could understand him, either.

The drive was long, almost the entire distance from the top of Europe to the bottom, northern Germany to southern Italy; Lübeck to Naples and nearby Sorrento, with several compulsory tourist stops on the way. In one elongated day, we had driven down from Germany through Austria, crossed into Italy over the Brenner Pass and sometime after midnight finally stopped for a snooze in the car near the coliseum in Verona. I woke up to see a gigantic red poster pasted on a crumbly wall next to my car. *Vota Communista*, it proclaimed, complete with a yellow hammer and sickle. I decided this was not a good place to stick around so we left in a hurry.

65. St. Mark's Square, Venice

We drove to Venice, hopped on their version of a city bus, a *vaporetto,* and cruised the canals to St. Mark's Square and the Bridge of Sighs. Venice didn't strike me as a place where I wanted to hang around. It was too dirty, too damp and riding the open *vaporettos* was just too damn cold. As we made our way from the main railway station to our car, we ran into an airline stewardess who said she was from New York and were we going to Rome? I'll pay for the gas, she volunteered. She wanted to see the Pope conduct the sunrise blessing on Easter morning. Of course, was our reply, so she grabbed her bag and followed us to the car. Rome was still a long drive south.

We drove most of the night through relatively mountainous terrain, and I managed to sleep a good part of the way down there, as Irv took over the wheel for a few hours and the stewardess, who wasn't much for conversation, slept soundly in the back seat along with our duffel bags and her suitcase. We stopped in a little mountain village late at night, and she graciously bought snacks, as we explained that we got gas dirt cheap courtesy of the U.S. Army.

Finally reaching the Eternal City early in the morning, I instantly really didn't care much for it. Too crowded and dirty and messy for my genteel taste buds. We dropped our passenger off somewhere near St. Peter's Square and stopped at the USO to get directions to a cheap hotel nearby. Then we got out our guidebook and did a lot of sightseeing, walking through ghostly ruins of the *Colosseum,* some of the nearby war and time ravaged Forum, which was basically crumbling bricks and columns and checking out the Pantheon, which in contrast to the other sites, was spotless and quiet and reverent and almost seemed like it was built just yesterday. St. Peter's, was on our list, but it was just too crowded to get into due to the approaching Easter.

Later, we even tossed some coins into the Fountain of Trevi, which to me was one of the most impressive things we saw, to insure our return to Rome, even though I wasn't real interested in returning.

That night, we were standing in front of a movie theater near our hotel waiting for the first show to end when another of the most beautiful girls I had ever seen popped out the door. She was more spectacular than Nancy from Nice - and I had thought that wasn't possible. She was Indian, with a little dab of red on her forehead, dark-skinned, long, perfectly black hair held in place with a red band, and a stylish short two-piece red suit. I only saw her for a few seconds as she walked right past us, crossed the sidewalk, hopped into a little red Alfa Romeo sports car and drove away. She was breathtaking and, of course, I never saw her again. She was a true lady in red. Well, actually, some hours later after the movie, as we were walking back to our hotel, I did see her toodling down the street in her bright red Alfa. Of course, she didn't see me. It wouldn't have mattered, anyway.

After a night of fitful sleeping on a lumpy mattress, in a noisy room that varied from way too hot to way too cold, the day finally dawned and I still wasn't too impressed with Rome. Irv and I ate a hasty breakfast and continued on with our half-hearted investigations. There had to be something here we could remember. And enjoy.

66. St. Peter's Square

67. Fountain of Trevi

An hour or so later, we sauntered into a relatively small church, *San Pietro in Vincoli*, to see one of Michelangelo's sculptures. The church had a sign on it, *"chiuso,"* that meant it was closed, but since no one was around, we just walked in. Towards the far end of the church, actually the front, but called the apse, of all things, we found the nearly eight foot tall version of Michelangelo as Moses that had just come back from an eyeball to eyeball chat with God. In his cold stone hands, Moses protectively held a tablet with the original written version of the Ten Commandments etched into it. The sculpture was sharply tilted and precariously perched on a pile of sand and stones from an excavation under the marble floor. I supposed they were looking for early Roman artifacts or possibly they were installing much needed plumbing.

Even to my uneducated eyes, I could tell this was an awesome work of art, and I couldn't believe that it was just dumped there like some cast-off old bath tub. Nobody was around so we got a chance to tread around in ancient dirt and boldly run our hands over the smooth hard blue-white marble. Even the veins on Moses' hands and arms were feel-able. If we had the tools, we could have carted off the whole thing and nobody would have missed it for days.

What a coup that would have been, but since Moses was bigger than my car, we reluctantly left without him. It was time to think about heading south for Naples. Being in Rome at Easter time might be a good thing for many people, many, many people, but not for us. The city was literally packed from one end to the other, and it was a struggle to get from anywhere to anywhere else. Besides, we had seen what we wanted to see and were already bored with the infinite variety of victory arches, round nightmare traffic "squares" and never knowing quite where we were on streets definitely not made for modern times. Or Easter weekend, for sure. We decided it would be wise to get out of town before the crowds completely shut down the already partially-paralyzed city. During the entire week before Easter we would probably be the only car leaving Rome.

The way out of Rome must have been the result of some Roman highway engineer's really bad nightmare. Although we left in the late morning, we didn't actually get out of the city of

Rome until mid afternoon. The roads were marked only with signposts that pointed in every which way, including up and down. We drove around and around one traffic circle for what seemed like hours; it offered about a dozen roads leading into parts unknown and finally we just said to hell with it and picked one. We ended up going for miles on a bumpy, rock-strewn, and cobble-stoned ancient Roman highway called the Appian Way. These early Italians may have been great engineers, but their roads were definitely not for modern vehicles - even one as tough as my little VW. I could imagine how bone-shaking it must have been for people riding in chariots or carts with steel-clad wheels. I could see why we were the only people on the road, and I got off it as soon as possible, before I wrecked my VW. Eventually we found a decent highway that actually led to Naples, our destination of the day.

Naples may have been the playground for ancient Roman emperors, but it was not a highlight and turned out to be even worse than Rome, without all the neat things to see. In fact, there weren't any neat things to see. The part that we saw was gray and industrial ugly and run-down and seemingly overrun by begging kids and whores. This was a big port for the U.S. Navy, and I felt a little sorry for the sailors who had to go on liberty there. At least we could leave.

After an uneasy night's snoozing in the car definitely well outside the city, leave we did. Bright and early the next morning, we hustled around the Bay of Naples, passed Herculaneum and Pompeii without a second thought, and got on one of the most romantic roads in Italy, according to our guide book. Well, someone had a different view of romance than I, for I found the last part of the road just plain scary, with it sharp curves and steep drop-offs. Sorrento did provide a shorter and quicker ferry ride to Capri, but looking straight down into the sea and jagged rocks on nearly every curve, I seriously doubted if it was worth the drive.

68. Ticket to Capri

We were happy when we finally got the VW parked on relatively flat ground and with us safely on board, the ferry slowly backed away from the dock. I fervently hoped my car would still be there when we returned. As the ship dieseled out of the port area, trailing a smokestack of dark smelly exhaust fumes, clear across the Bay of Naples to the north, we could see little answering wisps of smoke puffing out of Mt. Vesuvius. That gave me one more reason to worry about my car.

69. Mt. Vesuvius

The almost-an-hour ferry ride was pleasant, with not enough time passing to get truly sea sick and we docked on Capri around noon. As we walked down the long pier, I noticed two girls sunning themselves on a rock just off to the side so they became the first things we would check out.

The second thing was a visit to the Blue Grotto. We weren't quite sure what that was, but someone on the ship had told us it was a must see. But first things first. We walked over a row of slightly slippery rocks and quickly noticing the English-language Herald-Tribune, I offered the girls a couple of stale doughnuts we had left over from our last visit to the USO in Rome. They were Americans, busily composing letters to home. Outside of the stewardess who rode with us from Venice to Rome and didn't count, they were the first American girls I had seen or talked to in over a year. One of them drew me like a magnet; small, slender, dark hair with a tint of red, freckles, round-faced, sweet southern accent, delightfully cute and bordering on the beautiful. Her name was Carole Boucher and she was from Athens, Georgia. Her friend's name was Dickie, which I though was a strange name for a girl.

They graciously shared their thermos of coffee with us and let us browse through their newspaper while we chatted about our trip and they chatted about their trip. A quick check of our guidebook revealed that the Blue Grotto was a large cave that could only be entered from the sea and was noted for the fantastic color of its water. More interesting to us, there were niches carved into the walls that suggested the cave was a *nymphaeum,* a kind of boudoir for the Emperor Tiberius. The words nymph and boudoir whetted our interest a bit. The girls had already seen the grotto so they pointed out a nearby pier where we could hire a boat complete with the necessary oarsman. We reluctantly left to take a look at this marvel of nature and the Romans, but only after the girls promised to wait there until we returned. I was really, really, hoping they would be girls of their word and would actually be there when we returned. I was becoming experienced enough with the ways of femininity to hold my breath just a little bit. That cute little dark-haired Georgia girl had completely dazzled me in just a few short minutes. I hoped our excursion wouldn't take too long.

After settling on what we hoped was a fair price, we hopped into a small shaky rowboat that was propelled by a stout oarsman who took us skillfully about a mile down the coastline. We stopped once near another small boat and the fisherman, actually an octopusman, held up a small octopus that he had just caught. I snapped his picture and after a few minutes so our oarsman could catch his breath, we continued on our way.

70. Octopusman

Outside the entrance to the cave, we had to wait in line while other small boats entered and left the cave. It took some time as the entrance was only about three feet high and the rowboats had to wait until the waves were just right before they could make their mad dash to the interior.

Finally, it was our turn and we ducked down in the boat and entered into an amazing sight. The light inside the cave made the water glow a brilliant shimmering blue and as we splashed the gleaming water with our hands, it turned an iridescent blue-silver. There was no doubt in my mind that it was worth the trip, girls or no girls, Rome or no Rome. After about five minutes we had to leave and I never did see the make-out niches of Tiberius, but I imagined what a blast it would have been to swim naked in that water.

Carole and Dickie were still there when we returned.

71. Roman ruins on Capri

We gathered up all their stuff and walked past some crumbling ancient Roman ruins to a small *trattoria* for a quick plate of spaghetti and some bread and coffee. Time passed quickly as it was entirely pleasant to talk to someone at a normal rate without having to worry if they understood what you were saying. Right from the start, I liked this Carole girl a lot and from the flirting and banter, it was obvious that she liked me, as well. Her soft accent cut through my heart like melted butter.

With a bit of panic, I realized that the last ferry back to Sorrento was departing shortly. The girls were staying overnight and would be going to the mainland and taking the train back to Paris the next day. With Carole's phone number and address scribbled on an old envelope and stuffed into my billfold, we solemnly promised to meet in Paris in three days. Then Irv and I sprinted for the ferry.

72. Leaving the Isle of Capri

Back at the dock on the mainland, I was relieved to find my car still in place, untouched, and was that volcanic ash on the roof? We immediately started the long drive around that miserable bay and up the coast, deciding to sleep in the car when we finally got tired, which didn't take long. We by-passed Rome to the west and finally pulled into a small village named Tarquinia, found the city square and parked under a spreading orange tree for the evening. There was a small bar/hotel right behind the tree so we decided to check in and actually slept fully horizontal, for a change.

The next morning we were on our way before sunrise, almost refreshed but now driving with a purpose. However, the lure of the Leaning Tower of Pisa pulled us off the major highway for about an hour while we took the necessary touristy pictures. We tilted the camera to make the tower seem like it was straight and then took several where the subject, Irvin and then me, seemed to be leaning against it, holding it up with his hands. I discovered it was really impossible to get a "straight" tower since the upper floors seemed to be even more bent, I supposed in an early effort to make it appear straight. The end result was that the Leaning Tower should actually be called the Giant Banana or more to the point, the Enormous Erection.

73. Giant Banana of Pisa

We left Pisa in the late afternoon, and counting pit stops and slowing up for Genoa, we made pretty good time to the French border. About two a.m. and we were on one of those windy roads high above the Mediterranean again. Irv was driving. I dozed off only to awaken to the squeal of tires, a sickening metallic thud, and a look at a cliff wall about two inches from my face. Rounding a curve too fast, Irvin had lost control of the VW and smacked the rear fender into the cliff wall. Damn!

Ah, well, it wasn't serious and the car could easily be repaired. Feeling lucky that he lost control on the cliff side of the road and not the other side where it was about a thousand feet to the sea, I decided I had better take over the wheel for the rest of the night. We drove through Nice before the sun rose and I briefly thought of Nancy. It would be nice to surprise her, but I didn't remember where she lived. Anyway, thanks to the conditions put forth during the era of the Tower of Babel, that was over. We just couldn't communicate. At least that should be no problem with Carole.

CHAPTER 21: North to Paris and beyond and back to Paris

The road began to curve northward. Some miles north of Marseille, in a slightly higher inland elevation, it grew chilly with just a touch of snow in the air. We drove past a huge American war cemetery with perfectly aligned rows and rows of white crosses that were covered with white snow and I took a picture out of the window. I felt that was the least I could do; without these guys' sacrifice, I would probably have been more fluent in German. Way more.

74. The Cemetery

The road was much better, now. Not so many curves, so Irv and I just kept driving until we got tired enough to cat-nap in the car. We finally reached Paris without further accident. Thank God. It was early in the morning and cars and trucks were jamming up on the big ring road that circumnavigates Paris. Welcome to the big city. The traffic was worse than Rome's. After inching our way several miles, or since we were in France, several kilometers, in the pack, enough was enough. Since we didn't know where we were anyway, it definitely was time to get the hell out of this nightmare and go buy a map.

Finally around ten a.m. we checked into the American Church, which rented bunks in a barracks-like atmosphere for next to nothing. We did the usual shit, shower and shave, and Irv decided to crash and then take off by himself for a look around the city and to find out if he could actually converse with real French people. I decided to look for 3 *Rue du General Foy*, which was Carole's address. I hopped into my VW and noticed the little wing vent window on the passenger side was pushed in. Damn! Someone had broken into my car and I had left my camera in the glove box. However, I quickly checked and my camera was still there. I noticed some papers strewn on the floor and checking through them noticed that my gas coupons were gone. Damn again! Now I'd have to chase around to get more coupons or else buy gas on the open market which would cost me a fortune. The coupons were issued at the French border and allowed foreigners to buy gas at a reasonable price. Probably because we weren't supposed to be there, our U.S. Army coupons wouldn't work in France. Well, at least the thieves had the courtesy to leave my personal stuff alone. Welcome to Paris. The scumbags broke into my car the minute we walked into the church, and it wasn't even lunchtime yet.

75. Oh well, getting *"benzin"* in France wasn't really that bad

76. Relief; Paris pissoir (pissotières)

Live and learn. I left Irv to his own wishes and went off to find something to eat and then mount the search for Carole. Luckily, I had passed map reading in basic training and found her apartment on Rue du General Foy with little trouble. Well, maybe a little.

It actually wasn't her apartment; she got room and board in a French family's apartment along with Dickie and one other girl who, strangely enough, just like an old-time primary reading book, was named Jane. All she needed to complete the picture was a dog named Spot. Carole introduced me to her landlady, a crotchety old crone who didn't speak a word of English. Well, I had enough of that with Nancy from Nice so it was nothing new. Anyway, I wasn't there to see her.

Carole insisted on a quick tour of the apartment and a peek at their central courtyard, which substituted for a yard, a foyer and a parking lot, all in one, and then we were off to check out the city. Dickie and Jane, see ya later.

A couple hours passed quickly, driving, walking, talking and eating. It was a most pleasant experience, seeing Paris through the eyes of someone who actually lived there, and someone who spoke my language and the native tongue fluently.

We spent most of the time in neighborhoods off the beaten tourist track and the quiet part of the early evening was spent strolling along a quay on the River Seine, watching the barges and tour boats glide by. We watched the sun go down behind the Eiffel Tower. Now, in contrast to the rocky road around the bay, that was truly romantic. We stopped at a small store, a *boulangerie*, bought a loaf of bread, some cheese and, in honor of Carole's home state, also bought some warm Coca Cola. We sat in the car on the street near her rooming house and ate and talked until well past midnight. Finally it was time for a brief kiss goodnight and that was it. Now I had to follow the drunken cow paths called Parisian streets back to the American church and my lonely cot. Carole was impressive. Sweet and impressive. And nice. It was a long time before I fell asleep.

The next day was already here, and Irv and I needed to get back to Lübeck soon or we'd be listed as AWOL and promptly booted out of town. There was only time for a quick run into Carole's place and after a last long hug and much promising to write and make plans to meet again, hopefully in Brussels at the World's Fair, it was time to hit the road and drive like hell clear to northern Germany and home. Good by, Carole. I didn't really know her, but I knew I would miss her. At least for a while.

CHAPTER 22: High Jinks and Being Army

Although is was hard to remember that we were members of America's finest, occasionally, we did actually do something to be proud of - army-wise.

As told by James Bell (detachment CO during my stay).

We were on a field exercise, Sabre Hawk, with a small group of men I had selected from the detachment. We were pitted against a tough aggressor force simulating the Russians. On the last day of the exercise, almost the last hour, we were holding a command meeting in a tent, discussing the relative merits of the exercise. The Colonel, a big shot from Frankfurt, who was in charge said, "This would have been a perfect exercise except for the fact that we couldn't locate that damn Russian atomic cannon." Just as the words fell out of his mouth, one of my men, a DF'er, slithers into the tent and whispers in my ear.

"Sir," I promptly relayed the message, "we just found it".

Needless to say, our band of merry men from Lübeck won the best company award. Not bad for a bunch of fraternity guys.

Myron Havis:

On one field exercise, we wanted to make sure morale stayed high, so we made a beer run into the closest dorf. We loaded up the Jeep's trailer. On the last night of the exercise, I believe Captain Haber had rounded up some special food, ham or such, and we had something of a party. That almost proved costly, because in the middle of the night the heater in our squad tent got so hot that we came close to burning it down. Our return to battalion headquarters was also memorable. As entertainment while driving, we had run speakers from the radio huts on the 3/4 ton trucks in the cabs and connected them to the AM receivers, which were set to Radio Luxembourg and cranked. I'll never forget driving past the MP's at the main gate of Rothwesten with the rock-n-roll blaring and seeing the cover on the trailer with cases of empty beer bottles flapping and revealing the contraband. Fortunately, we got through without any repercussions.

77. Company of fine gentlemen, Christmas, 1957: L to R: J. Moran, Me, M. Kehrli, J. Young with glasses, M. Scott, I. Deranger, D. Ade, standing; unknown, H. Walthall

Bob Fleming:

The Christmas I remember most vividly is a Christmas spent in Lübeck... There was a displaced persons camp located next to Mutti's. The camp was a temporary refuge for families who managed to escape East Germany by crossing the nearby border. We thought it would be nice to buy clothes for the kids at the camp as Christmas gifts. We mentioned this to Mutti and she suggested that instead of buying clothes we should have a Christmas party at our house and give them toys. She said that they had plenty of clothes which were donated by different charitable organizations. We took Mutti's advice and held the party. I had the honor of being "Der Weihnachtsman" (Santa Claus). As each child came up to get his or her gift they would sing a little song or recite a poem and then return to their seat and open their present. I noticed one little girl who didn't open her gift, and asked Mutti to see if something was wrong. She talked to her and then told me that the little girl said that her mother was sick back at the camp and couldn't come with her.

She told Mutti that the wrapped present was the most beautiful thing she had ever seen and she wanted her mother to see it before she opened it because she knew her mother had also never seen anything so beautiful. The party ended with everyone standing around the Christmas tree singing "Stille Nacht" (Silent Night). There wasn't a dry eye amongst a bunch of macho GI's some three thousand miles from home who were experiencing the true meaning of Christmas.

Mort Weston:

Brownie grew in disfavor and drank too much. I worked with him in the beginning when we were on the hut trucks. He would be too drunk to take code during our work schedule and would sleep mostly. One evening Lt. Bell came to the site. Voice alerted us and I woke up Brown but to no avail. He had been sleeping with his face in the mill and he had the imprint of the letters all over his face when Bell walked in. That was the last straw, along with how he mistreated Bell's dog. Darius or Derus. Before he left Lübeck, Brownie was at the site and told me he was going to burn our outhouse down. He then proceeded to pour gas on it and set it on fire.

78. Bull Durham, Ingrid, Me, Kid

CHAPTER 23: Letters from Carole and then Brussels

April 28
Dear Don,

Didn't mean to start some sort of word warfare - the impediment I guess was an explanation for a misspelled word, I think. We sort of kid ourselves 'cause we can't even stammer sensibly any more, much less attempt to write.

Right now, the only bright sunny thing in this room is your letter. Am sitting at the moment in front of sooty casement windows watching the soft black radioactive clouds go by. It's a rainy Sunday afternoon with too much to do and no moving spirit to spur you on to greater things. But there's always the looking forward to good times in Brussels.

I wish I could come visit you in Lübeck - the local agencies sound fascinating for your descriptions were most vivid. I guess they'll always remain descriptions to me, as my grades would absolutely collapse to complete nothingness if I ever thought about leaving town again. You're so nice to ask and I wish more than anything it were possible, but my job next year definitely depends on the outcome of this year - am starting life as struggling young musician, and early May concerts determine degree which determine job - that's the story of my life - doesn't even fill half a page - but does explain absence from Lübeck.

Wish you were hear to witness the hunting season victims. The man of the house prides himself and his fame and subsequently can't see past his wild boar meals to watch his boarders suffer. Eventually one pays for European frolics and believe me we're paying in advance and in full. It's been a constant toss up between brain and boar for three days now. It's worse than a summer rain - it'll never let up.

Take care of yourself - must close - Steve Allen come on TV at seven and must get the barbecue going. Wish you were here to help - I always mess up on the sauce.

Love, Carole

May 8
Dear Don,

You look everywhere - in parks, around corners, in store windows, under beds, on top of tables, behind news racks... there's absolutely nowhere to find the words to categorize your last letter - an absolute work of art, my dear - even the Louvre couldn't find the right frame.

Our plans for Brussels are still swinging along on an unnamed star - now we're trying to rent a car for less than $10 and are having nearly no luck. We figure this is the only way to go, since we'll probably be sleeping in it, too. It sounds from your letters as if you're staying for a long time. My wallet, which is attached to my French mother's juggler vein, says I can only stay a couple days - wish I had had the luck to have a boy's name so I could take a thirty day leave.

Made final arrangements for long boat ride home today. Don't know about you, but am beginning to feel some questions mixed in with the anxious. As much as I'll be glad to move from gloomy household, I still hate to leave Paris. I think it's really going to be rather hard for both of us. Just tell me who in the world is going to care (besides your family) whether you went to Capri and ate doughnuts in the rain or not? We're going to have to do lots of writing next year. I can see that - of course, responding party will find it hard taking his eyes off the pretty college co-eds long enough to write to dazed piano plugging-choral directing friend who by this time will be long lost in the sea of hallowed humanity. Banality has become a forté here so I'll quit.

Choosing to meet in the Russian Embassy by Lenin's picture really isn't too good of an idea - well to each his own, but I'm gonna be at the Atomium - don't know what I'll meet there - but if I have my Italy luck, I'd do better to stay in Paris.

Just kidding my favorite German, of course - sense of humor is so worn out I hate myself - not much better when feeling is reversed - so you'll have to force a smile in spite of yourself.

Bye - hope you had a nice Spring, my beginning was a little dark - no Yankee sun in Paris; but there hope of one in May!
Love, Carole Jo

May 17
Dear Don,

You're too much, my boy, sending that money is the sweetest gesture in the world but one also that I couldn't possibly accept. You had really saved my life, as I didn't think the check for the month would get here in time, but Daddy heard my call and came through. I seem to always be boring you with these problems - somehow we manage to get by, though - one thing I will accept is your thoughtfulness. At the same time I hope you don't tag me as ungrateful 'cause you know I appreciate it. I'd feel much happier if you'd take it and buy something for yourself - something you've wanted for a long time - like a baseball diamond where every hit's a home run. We'll see what we can find for you at Brussels - hey, just 8 more days.

Oh, Don, today's a bad day. We're having lots of rains, high winds, and communists. At the minute, the whole town has gone on strike plus the accompaniment of 10 or 20 street riots. Don't mean to be a sensationalist, but this has certainly gotten to be a drama. Of course this has been happening all year but it's the first time we've been officially ordered to stay in the house until it more or less blows over. How these people can endure this year after year, I'll never know. No wonder the French are frivolous and carefree and irresponsible. They have to grab each moment of temporary peace they can find and make the most of it. It's just so sad... all this continuous fear and instability. I just had a long talk with Madame in the house here - she's a good representative of the people in general; pitifully reconciled but still hopeful. It seems to me the only way out again will be through force and I shudder to think that I really don't think they could possibly endure another war.

At the moment, I'm an easy prey for the claws of sentimentality. The trip to Brussels is the shot in the arm - if it weren't for that, I might climb in my already packed trunk along with all the other anxious articles. Yes I do lots of talking, Don - I want to go just as bad as you do - as far as giving Europe back to the Indians - well, I'm afraid it would just be a down payment; even for them.

Attribute it to the out-dated calendar plus an inadequate mind but I don't know what I was thinking about when I said the

23rd. We couldn't possibly come until the 24th as we have school through Friday. We've found an old Citroen, that doesn't even have room for zippers any more, which will be our means of transportation. It's understandable that you probably already have plans for the 24th - if not, then I'd still like to look for the Atomium with the blonde under it. If your plans have changed then feel free to say forget it or else reassure that the A. building will still be there the 24th. I'll go out and eat weeds if it isn't.

And by the way, you're lucky - our sun doesn't even take the time to see if it's raining. I don't think it would know what to do if it wasn't. One thing you must promise me - we won't succumb to bridge if it's still raining when you're here. It's such a defeatist's admittance (i.e. a formal way of saying I don't play.)

Sorry you had to insult your intellect on this letter by wasting its time. The day has done nothing to invoke inspiration - but am thinking about you and the sun you're going to bring.

Love, Carole

May 22
Dear Don,

This one's gonna be quick - am en route to class and must also give myself plenty of time to run through the rioting crowds and confront 35 million policemen - other than that, everything's pretty dull.

Paris is having its share of the German rain and speaking of Paris.. there are rumors that American soldiers aren't allowed inside the portals anymore - from whence does this news cometh and is it spoken with an honest tongue? The Army has no right to ruin our holiday - must be a strict outfit you're in - a mean leader, too - well, I hope it's just some hearsay.

Am still planning on seeing you Saturday afternoon - but one thing worries me - how will I know you? It's been a long time, you know, and cold weather does bad things to my memory - wear your uniform if you want, but for goodness sake, leave that parachute at home.. Don, sometimes you just don't understand...

Anyway the time I spend writing only augments the amount of time for this to get there. Meet me on the heather by the old stone gate, Saturday around 3:00.

Rebecca

Early in the afternoon, after a speedy trip down from Lübeck, Dick Nelson and I had been lucky enough to find a farm house with rooms to rent within a loud shout from the main gate of the Fair. We had rented a room in the attic and put another upstairs room on hold for Carole and, supposedly, Dickie. We drove the few hundred yards to the gate, and I wandered around in the drizzle for a while before taking refuge in the American pavilion and pausing to check out the models as they paraded the latest American fashion down a long ramp. I thought they were ok, but nothing in comparison with Carole, of course. Just taller. Nellie had gone off by himself, and planned to spend most of the afternoon and night drinking beer in the Benelux pavilion.

The rain increased to a steady downpour and shortly before three o'clock, I staked out a semi-dry spot near the entrance to the Atomium, the huge shiny dripping wet aluminized version of an iron molecule gone berserk. Taller than a football field standing on end, it certainly wouldn't be hard to find. Three o'clock sharp: no Carole. I waited and watched, eyes straining through the rain, but she didn't show up. Four o'clock sharp: no Carole. At five o'clock, still no Carole and I finally said to hell with it and trotted miserable, frustrated and sopping wet back to my trusty VW. Surely something must have happened.

It was about a ten second drive back to the muddy field/parking lot next to the guest house. Just enough time to think all sorts of dire thoughts about the fickle opposite sex. I was thankful to be alone.

I was sloshing toward the house when a tiny, beat up, gray French-looking car with a sliding canvas top pulled into the field, lurching and belching fire as it came near, skinny tires spinning furiously through the mud. I backed away cautiously, not knowing what to expect. As the rolling junk heap pulled up to me, the bottom half of the driver's side window flipped open and I heard a sweet feminine southern voice say, "Do you speak English? Would you happen to know where we could rent a room for the night?" It was Carole. Unbelievable. God had a sense of humor, after all.

Talking a mile a minute as we sat at the table in the suddenly cozy kitchen, Carole wound down as she explained how she and Dickie had borrowed someone's old Citroen *Deux Chevaux,* which had something like a slightly overgrown lawnmower engine and the reputation of being nearly indestructible. It was France's answer to Germany's VW Beetle and being typically French, one thing after another had gone wrong with the car, and they had spent a good deal of time driving at half the normal maximum speed of 50 miles per hour while wearing out their wrists cranking the manually-operated windshield wipers. They had stopped several times to ask for help, but the car was too far gone for a quick fix. Basically, they were told, it probably needed a new engine. Coming in on a wing and a prayer suddenly took on new meaning.

79. The Atomium, Brussels

By the time Carole calmed down, and I was into dry clothes, dusk had come and gone. The rain stopped and the moon and stars made their appearance. Either through pre-planning or thoughtfulness, Dickie conveniently decided she was soooo tired that she would stay in their room and get a good night's sleep. With our combined five languages, French, Flemish, Dutch, German, and English, the four of us we managed to ask our host if he would try to locate someone to patch the Two Horses jalopy together. He graciously agreed and Carole and I decided to walk over to The Fair. Our first stop would be the Atomium.

From my earlier trip to The Fair, I knew that many pavilions, with their soft lights and colored water falls, cast a magical glow over the fairy-tale landscape and the scene at night was more enjoyable and much more romantic. This was the way I dreamed it would be. Almost like a movie. And we were the stars.

Most of the major exhibitions closed early, but the restaurants and bars and a few die-hard exhibitions were open virtually all night. The Atomium had dozens of small windows cut into each huge silver ball and was rather bold and stark by day. However, at night, flashing patterns of light sparkling through these openings created the illusion of an actual gigantic electron. Unfortunately, we couldn't get in to take the elevator to the top so we settled for a bratwurst and visited the small Czech pavilion, which I had discovered was one of my favorites, with a particularly stunning and colorful exhibit.

80. Atomium at night

Earlier tensions and frustrations disappeared as we caught the aerial tramway, which was like a ski lift with small four-man gondolas, for a long, slow tour of the entire site. At this time of night, the tram was virtually deserted, so we had the privilege of snuggling in entirely alone as we glided silently over and through and under some of the most striking buildings I had ever seen. I decided I would get wet and miserable and frustrated every day if they all could end like this.

After several loops around the fairground, which were relatively compact considering the nature of the exposition, we decided this night actually had to end so we trooped happily back to the farm house. It was hard to believe I would actually be sleeping with Carole, but she would be one floor beneath me.

Morning came too soon and I was worried that Nellie hadn't come home. I checked the car and, sure enough, he was blissfully passed out in the front seat. After we ate a huge breakfast, we decided to make a quick tour of some of the major pavilions in the morning and then head for Paris as soon as the Citroen was able. Although it was Sunday, our host had found someone to look at the 2 CV, as Carole called it, along with some other less endearing terms, but we needed to get it to his garage early in the afternoon. So dragging Dickie and a protesting and semi-sick Dick along, we virtually ran through the exhibitions of the U.S., France, Germany, and holding my breath, that I wouldn't be grabbed, Russia. The star of the fair, the Phillips Pavilion, was a tent-like structure designed by someone named Le Corbusier and had 400-some odd speakers playing weird electronic music by some Frenchman named Varese. Too much for me, and I wasn't sure Carole, a musician, liked it either. The morning hours flew by all too quickly, but I liked the company - at least the part of it named Carole.

81. French Pavilion

The 2 CV, which according to Carole was actually short for *Deux Chevaux Vapeurs,* or two steam horses, didn't run perfectly, but it did run. Apparently a spark plug had blown out, or up, and the old gray heap had chugged along for miles on only one cylinder. Since I had a week more of leave time, we decided I would drive along behind the *Chevaux* all the way to Paris and if it just conked out again, we would just push it into the ditch and continue on our way. Nellie was now too hung over to drive and Dickie couldn't, so Carole and I became the designated drivers. Not exactly how I would have planned it, but I would have more time to spend with her in Paris.

The next few days passed in a hazy blur. Carole was off to class, I sent Nellie back to Lübeck on the train - that'll teach him to drink - and I spent a lot of time sleeping late and just hanging around the city taking colored slides. Although I really wasn't into the art scene, I decided to visit the Louvre. About six hours later, I stumbled out into the street, and nearly walked in front of a taxicab, as my mind was totally overloaded by what I had seen inside. I wondered if this was what art supposed to do and was I missing something?

One day while I was wandering around, I bought a Jackie Gleason Orchestra record and then spent several hours on the Eiffel Tower, going clear to the uppermost observation deck. I gave a brief thought about walking down, but it was a long, long way and it looked like it could be a little dizzying. I gave her the record that evening and we sat and listened to it. I wasn't sure she really liked the music - it was more than a little maudlin - but I was positive she appreciated the thought.

82. View from Eiffel Tower

As soon as Carole was free after classes, we visited another part of town, usually buying cheap snacks, and just walking around enjoying each other's company and soaking in the atmosphere. I knew I could really get to like this.

The night before I had to leave for Lübeck, we decided to load up on bread and cheese and warm Coke and drive willy-nilly through the streets to the Eiffel Tower so we could sit underneath it in the park and have a late night picnic.

As the clock wound past nine o'clock, pleasantness turned to fright as we turned a corner on *Rue Soufflet* leading to the French Pantheon. Storming around the corner of this giant tomb for French notables and headed directly toward us was a wild, screaming mob of Parisians. At least we assumed they were French citizens. But what kind? Crazy, angry Communists or someone else equally crazed? We didn't hang around to find out, and before we were swallowed by the mob, I did a quick U-turn and got the hell out of there.

Several blocks away we slowed down enough so Carole could lean out of the car window and ask some passersby what was going on. Oh, they said, De Gaulle has taken over. He's going to head a new government. Well, that's good news, I think, Carole said and we continued on our way.

We crossed the Seine on our way to the Eiffel Tower. One small mistake. The *Champs Elysees* was absolutely jammed with thousands of singing, shouting, celebrating people going slightly nuts with the joy of the moment. In order to get to the Eiffel Tower, it was necessary to get across that broad avenue, which was virtually impossible. It was a no-brainer. We followed several other cars as they slowly pulled into the crowd, and I slid the folding roof back so Carole could stand on the seat and join in the shouting. Viva De Gaulle! Viva De Gaulle!

Here's this German car with US Forces plates and a screaming American girl hanging out the top inching down the *Champs Elysees* and nobody noticed us. Thankfully. The crowd and the cars and the noise thinned as we circled around the *Arc de Triomphe* once and headed south down the *Avenue Kléber,* crossed the Seine on the *Pont d'Iéna* and found a parking spot practically under the Eiffel tower. We walked past one of the huge tower legs and found a handy park bench almost completely surrounded by bushes. It was totally quiet and peaceful and we were finally alone. And starving. The bread and cheese didn't last long and even though I hated warm Coke, I managed to choke down half a bottle. It would be nice to say that because of the excitement of the evening, we then made out like bandits, but, unfortunately, that didn't happen. We sat and talked, serious stuff, like what was the future of Carole and Don, and if there was even to be one.

83. Champs Elysees before the demonstration

84. Eiffel Tower at night

We were both caught in the magic of Paris, the magic of the World's Fair. Capri. Our times together were so totally extraordinary, what would we be like in a "normal" situation, if one existed. We didn't really know that much about each other, our families, our backgrounds, our plans. Was our whole existence together based on hormones and geography? Truly scary stuff as neither of us knew the answers and we knew we would find none. At least not at that moment.

We finished off the bread and almost got the pants scared off us as a tall gendarme, with a round cap and dark cloak came sauntering by and told us it was maybe not a good idea to be here so late at night. There wasn't much to disagree with so we took his advice, walked back to the car and wound our way back across the Seine, through the now empty *Place de la Concorde* and straight north to Carole's apartment. I felt strange, knowing that this might be the last night I would ever see her, and I'm sure she felt the same, as she was strangely quiet on the ride home. After one long, slow, painful kiss, she ran into the apartment, with tears streaming down her face.

Real men don't cry. I did.

One last night on the cot at the American Church and I was off to Lübeck. A few days later I received another letter.

June 1
Dear Don,
    This has certainly been a nite to remember. Saying goodbye to our family was no easy job - despite our many complaints, the good times have been just as numerous and just as unforgettable as the other kind.
    As you very well know, I'm absolutely no good in a parting scene - have never been able to play the part. This past week was one that no playwright could reproduce. I saw Paris for the first time with someone who half way understands the Europeans and thinks a little as I do. Don, I loved every minute of the time that you were here. I know I did nothing to show any sort of appreciation for the time you took with me but I hope in some small way you know that Paris to me was at its most beautiful.

There was not much time for explaining to you many things which I should have - but frankly, I was scared. You mentioned the fact that last hour, of people and situations and what are the relations among the two. In reality they should be of two different categories but at present they are not. It's all a question of really knowing your own mind - something I've yet to grow up to. The one thing I do know is that experiences shared together are the things which hold people together. Our short excursions (together) in Europe, shall never be forgotten; by me at least. How much importance should be placed on the setting is up to the author - and if the author is a prolific one, he'll write a sequel and maybe this time in the United States.

Lots of times writers prefer to share their success with one novel only for fear that the others may be failures... but whatever he chooses to do, it will be what he wants, he himself. Am really making no sense at all - it's late and I'm afraid if I go on I'll write something even Morse himself couldn't decode.

I loved Paris in the Spring – by the way, it rained Friday. The tower's still there but the first prize exhibit isn't.

Love,
Carole

What a lovely letter.

And

Yes, the song is true.

85. April in Paris; twilight

CHAPTER 24: Back to Almost-normal: Christiana

It was hard to get Carole out of my mind, but it was only too obvious that facts were facts and she was in Paris and I wasn't. Our only hope of getting to know each other, at least a little bit, was by mail. I looked forward to receiving her letters, but it seemed like she was running hot and cold and I didn't know what to make of it. I did know that I really missed her.

A cute little blonde changed all that. Late one afternoon, as I was coming back from the store on the corner, swigging on a half-liter bottle of chilled Coke and munching on a bar of Tablerone chocolate, I passed two young ladies and offered them a chunk of my chocolate. I was surprised when they accepted. We all continued walking towards our house, alternately eating candy and drinking pop and trying to make small talk in bad English and German. The usual, what's your name, are you an Ami? What do you do and all that. When we reached the gate to #10, I didn't make a move to go in, but just kept on walking with the girls towards the little park on the corner. They were surprised and started giggling. Were they out trolling for GI's or what?

At the park entrance, the girls stopped and shook hands good-by and one turned and walked down the street. This left me with the blonde, and I managed to ask her in my broken German if it was ok to walk her home. She nodded and we walked into the park. I felt real good walking with her - almost like we belonged together. About halfway through the park was the landing for the little ferry boat that crossed the *Wakenitz*, back and forth, all day. We sat on a bench and watched it for a little while and then she indicated that she had to get on home. Preferably, from this point, alone.

Before she left, though, we agreed to meet the next day at the same time right here on the same bench by the ferry landing. When I got back to the house, I immediately ran up to my room and got out my Berlitz German language book. It was time to get serious about this stuff. Her name was Christiana.

Now what? I was in the proverbial pickle with emotions running both ways. Was I some sort of wishy-washy fool or was I acting like any normal hot-blooded American boy. This was a totally new experience for me. I had met this really nice American girl that seemed to like me as much as I liked her and now this German *fraülein* comes along and spoils all that. My heart was in Paris, but my body was in Lübeck. Did I go to the park bench or stay away? Would she be there or not? There was only one way to find out.

86. The *Wakenitz* Ferry

She was there. The little ferry was also there, so we hopped aboard and settled in for the short ride. On the other side of the *Wakenitz,* which in actuality is sort of a combination river/lake, were shops, stores, apartment blocks, boat rentals, an Opel dealership, and a really nifty little garden, with statues, benches, arbors and flowers of all kinds and colors. The walks were pea gravel and crunched as we strolled, like an old married couple, admiring the blossoms and keeping conversation to a minimum. It was quiet, peaceful, and, with this girl, sort of a magical place.

I was heading for something, but I was not quite sure just what. I knew it would be something good.

87. Arbor in the park across the *Wakenitz*

I

88. Statue in the arbor

144

June 6

Dear Don,

 De Gaulle's in power – no more riots – only beautiful summery days left – oh well, you gotta chose your demonstrations and it's no fun when the weather's perfect.

 We're staying here the rest of our days – have canceled trip to Lausanne as we are now recuperating from broken spinal cords after long hard move out of the General Foy home. The departure was touching – our last view glimpsed Madame counting the May's rent, Monsieur flogging the children and German girl cleaning up American boarder's room as it was well submerged in dust and old champagne bottles – uh – bottle. The famous fifth was finished by Dickie and cohorts and was preceded by lengthy, praiseworthy speech for selfless donor.

 So.o.o.o, why don't you come back to Paris? It's worth the long drive cause it means retakes of the silhouettes I ruined and also a new place I discovered yesterday. It's sort've a cave-like place where everyone sits around and drinks a coffee while these three professional guitarists play classical and French folk songs.

 There's no drinking or rough sailors – just this quite beautiful music – it's a Switzerland type atmosphere with the charm of France. Okay you can go ahead and say I told you so – but I do miss you, I'd say more but I'm afraid these letters will get published.

 Two weeks ago it was your birthday and I got a box of candy – as well as I can remember, back in the States the procedure is usually reversed. Maybe I could buy you some fried chicken, hush puppies, and green peas and rice, on your way home from the war – do you come my way?

 Let's see now – maybe if I mentioned a drought – no – that'd never work – or – oh heck, I give up – just come!

Carole

Christiana was a gem. A true Germanic queen. Blonde hair streaked with brown, or vice versa, rounded rosy cheeks, soft and cuddly, with a smile from here to there. Not really beautiful in the traditional movie-star sense, but then again, maybe she was. Hands down, I found her to be one of the most pleasing and pleasant people I had ever met and she liked me a lot. A real lot. And with my mind and feelings in a tizzy, I began to return the favor. Realizing that Carole was getting ready to board a ship for home gave me all the guilt-free permission I needed.

89. Christiana

The first few days, we saw each other as often as possible. Which wasn't enough to satisfy either one of us, but with my wacky work schedule, that was a part of life I couldn't change. She struggled with English, but was more competent with her foreign language that I was with mine. That just added to the charm, as we strolled through the parks and close neighborhoods sharing a German-American dictionary. Christiana was living in a townhouse with her *Grossmutter,* her grandmother. It was part of a much larger almost block-long grey concrete and wood facaded building located a few blocks past the little park where we met. The old lady, I assumed she was old since I never saw her, definitely was not to know about our little *tete-a-tetes.* I was

146

apparently in a situation of being one of the not-to-be-trusted and dreadful "Ami's." The first time Christiana allowed me to walk her to her door, she shussed me with an upraised finger. We talked for a few minutes in barely audible whispers and then, with exaggerated big steps, I tip-toed slowly away. I could see her grinning in the hall light as she opened the door - quietly.

During the time I was not with Christiana, my emotions were in total turmoil. Women weren't supposed to be such problems, were they? I knew I still had a lot to learn, especially about handling this emotional roller coaster. After getting a letter from Carole, I was torn between heading back to Paris for a day or two - especially since she sincerely seemed to want me to come back - or just getting on with life - Christiana - here in Lübeck. I was saved from making any dramatic decisions by the fact that I couldn't get any leave time, and my schedule was set in stone so there was no missing work or switching with someone for a few days. I was way too cowardly to go AWOL.

The letters from Carole and her sometime fuzzy allusions to a future, maybe together or not, seemed to keep me from falling ass over appetite for Christiana. I tried to get a sense of Carole's commitment, but it appeared that she was afraid and definitely hesitant to take such a bold step. I decided I really had no choice except to go with what was available right here and now and at this moment. Reluctantly. Or maybe not.

CHAPTER 25: Not Everyone is Well in Camelot

Mort Weston:

I celebrated my birthday in Lübeck with all the usual importance attached by Germans to birthdays. A few days afterward it was approaching swing trick time for the "kick ass" 058 Weston team to take over at Blankensee. I had never felt so ill in my life. I told Lt. Bell that I couldn't work, I was sick. Of course the sick and wounded had to be transported to a small British antiaircraft unit at Todendorf about 60 mi away. Lt. Bell decided to send me to the US hospital in Bremerhaven, but he decided since our truck ran by the German hospital to have them check me out.

I was taken to the internal medicine building and checked over by a German internist. He said he could find nothing wrong with me and to go to work, but he said, "Oh, I've forgotten to take your temperature." It was way the hell up there so that was the real clue he needed to stick me in a bed in a ward with about six other German patients.

Dr. Goades, an internal medicine resident, came into the room and he and all the other nurses and patients were fascinated that I was American and an opportunity to try out their English. To relieve the high fever Dr. Goades started pumping a large 250ml syringe full of liquid directly into the muscle of my forearm because he had missed the vein while he was concentrating on speaking Oxford English.

I was yelling from the pain and the large amount of fluid infused into my forearm. He was so embarrassed with his mistake and when he found out that I was a pre-med student we became friends while I was in Lübeck. Later I found out that I made more money as an E5 than he did as a resident doctor.

I was begging for a drink of water. Water was not on the menu neither was coke but dark beer was recommended. I said I'll take it. Even in a dehydrated state I could not drink that warm beer. I heard a voice across the room, "If you're not going to drink that beer, can I have it?" My German was good enough to understand him and I told him I was really sick and he said he wanted the beer anyway.

Lt. Bell found out that I was sick, not malingering in a hospital ward and started worrying about the situation. There was one of his troopers with a top secret- crypto clearance, a high fever, and being medicated by strange doctors. He decided that the proper action was to station another ASA buddy with me at the hospital until my brain reformed and all the dits and dahs stayed where they belonged.

After a few days the laboratory work showed that I had leptospirosis. This was a wicked bacteria usually found in cattle but could be transferred to humans. They checked the blood titer for this disease because they had some German border guards with the same illness. They explained the vector was probably mouse piss. Apparently, a thoughtless field mouse had peed on some food that I had eaten making every muscle in my body hurt, sapping my energy, and my brain shutting down some important functions. I really thought I was going to die.

It was finally decided to transfer me clear across Germany to the Bremenhaven army hospital in one of the voice guy's personal VW bug. He modified the back seat somehow so I could lie down. After about a week or so of misery and antibiotic injections, I was recovered enough to get sent back to Lübeck and the duty roster. But that was a God-awful experience I never want to repeat.

My brief bout with a bug.

Most of us stayed relatively healthy, being strong, sturdy, young studs and, besides, we didn't have enough time or energy to get sick. However, I caught some sort of flu, with diarrhea, fever, sweats, chills and all that good stuff. Since I was so sweaty, I decided to take a long hot bath to rinse off the smelly stuff. After soaking for about half an hour, I stood up to get out of the tub and promptly passed out wet and naked on the cold marble-tiled floor.

I awoke some minutes later, (hours?) woozy and shivering and went back to bed until the next day. I don't remember exactly, but I think Elsa, the maid, saw me lying there and covered me with a towel and helped me to my room. Being a good trooper, and patriotic to the core, I recovered completely in time to resume my important military duties on the next shift.

CHAPTER 26: Mixed Feelings

Tuesday, June 10
Dear Don,

Everything now is sort've blank - have never before had the experience of leaving a place, maybe for a lifetime. Things are so familiar now - my own ice cream store, dentist, bus... seems as if my family has been away visiting and not me? (I) Paris has done a fine job of getting me thoroughly confused as to what I want to do and even to what I think sometimes. Guess you feel the same way - I just keep thinking that after I get home, everything will fall into place - even the things such as thoughts, which are with you the whole time.

Why is it the things you really want to achieve always fall into place the month or the week that you've going to leave it? Your comprehension of German, for instance - perfect example. I wish I could get to the place where I could appreciate immediately and discipline myself to the adjustment - not spending so much time fighting it. I guess that when you grow up - and who wants to do that?

Frankness seems to be a (policy) (oh dear, policie) with us - one you don't "come by" very often. Am glad, ' cause that way no one is victim of false impressions which always lead to hurt feelings. I would like to give an intelligible answer to your letter but to, repeat the first paragraph, I'm putting off all difficult problems till I get home. I don't trust myself to think clearly here in Europe. Most people have become miraculously "saved" in France, so to speak, but to be childishly honest, I can't distinguish anymore between mood and stable ideas. You're probably saying to yourself, "this poor girl's getting worked up over nothing... who does she think she is?" But... before I left home I guess I gave myself too much credit for thinking I knew what I wanted - now, I don't know... it's like looking for the ace in a deck of jokers... And so the story goes........

I'm trying to think how the Volkswagen company can start paying you for driving their car.. have actually come up with no solution except for maybe a synchronized seeing-eye plastic cow bumper which works automatically. What do you think or have you wadded this up in disgust? Save it, it'll be good for some

blotting paper.. the book you're going to write, remember? Am
counting on that and from hearing from you soon... one June
morning.

> *With all the Paris sun and beauty*
> *I can muster up, with love -*
> *Carole*

From her last letter, it appeared that Carole and I were
riding on the same emotional roller coaster. Here she was,
getting ready to board ship for home and here I was,
unbeknownst to her, holding hands with Christiana. I had asked
her if I would be welcome to visit her - or more - when I got
home and she apparently couldn't make up her mind if that was
ok or not. So, I get the "I'm so confused here in Europe that I
can't think straight, but not only that, I'm also not sure about
what I want to happen" combined "with all the Paris sun and
beauty I can muster up, with love," No wonder I was going nuts.

And then I got:

1. Fol EM are rel asg orgn indicated and asg US Army Ret-
reasg Sta fr mil svc. AUTH: AR 635-250. EM WP to
Bremerhaven, Ger RUA to Staging Area prior to 0645 hrs. on
13 Jul 58 for processing and mov by US Govt surface vessel to
US. Ship: USS Butner. EDCSA sta asg. 1 Aug 58.

In plain English, these were my orders to ship home. I was to
be in Bremerhaven by 0645 on the 13th of July for shipment to
the US on the USS Butner. Joy. Not really. I had about a month
left in Lübeck and a lot on my mind.

In a brief conservation with the 1st Sergeant, I indicated my
fondest desire to follow those orders. As a parting shot at my
bluntness, he indicated I wouldn't be making Sergeant although
technically I was next on the promotion list. He told me that
since I was going home, I wouldn't need it. The stripes would go
to someone else. Well, so much for that. Aside from a blow to
my ego and last few paychecks, it meant I would have to pay for
the shipment of my car to New York.

Christiana, gentle soul, was a stabilizing influence. She didn't know about Carole, but I knew she could sense my hesitancy with her. She also knew that I would be going home sometime soon, but not exactly when and, quite likely, that would be the end of that. We didn't talk about it much. However, we kept on meeting as often as possible, and I even let her take me once in a while to a German movie in a German movie theater, complete with loud pipe organ and synchronized dancing colored water fountains. This theater was only a few blocks from her home, so we generally stopped at a *wurst* stand for a quick snack and then walked or rode a tram if one was available. She was reluctant to ride in my car, for whatever reason.

Letter from Carole
Tuesday, June 17
Dear Don,

There's not much time 'cause I'm fixin' to get shot with penicillin and presented with my 8th bowl for soup for supper - both of which I want to be prepared for.

Friday evening (13th), about the same time Charlie Brown dropped the ball, my appendix said, "C.J., I'm kind of this old world and this old life"..Was taking a walk in some nearby gardens when it flared up. In a most undramatic pass out scene, I did... and 1/2 hour later I was on a very French operating table (Louis XIV) in a very French hospital (Cistern Abbey style) from where I now write letter. It all happened so quickly there wasn't even time to have a few neighbors worry about you (usually the best part, they say.) Everything's been rather frantic, trying to change boat ticket, father trying to dry up the Atlantic, and me in the middle not being able to do a thing.

All in all, my doctors are very capable and friends have been unbelievably helpful. This will teach you to say, How are you? in your next letter. It's the first room I've had in France, however, which looks out upon the famous Paris skyline (I put it in small letters, trying to de-emphasize its importance in my life.)

Well, it's just about sailing time - sure hope Carole has a good trip! When are you ever going to be able to get out of your rather measured existence? Have orders come through yet? Wish you were working on my system - was really lucky to get a place the first of July on the Liberté. It's a very French name belonging to the Frenchiest of lines - but in actuality it's a steal from the Germans back in '44.

Try to get some sun, that is if the German girls in French bikinis don't detract from its powerful rays. As for having the "shakes" about leaving - you can always count on some Boucher luck... I have some to spare.

My 10 minute writing session is up - do try to understand brevity - will write later when nurses fall out of this regimented line around my room.

Love, Carole

Now what? Carole was missing an appendix and her boat ride home and, to top it off, she was stuck in some French hospital. There was no way I could get down there and provide some measure of comfort. And since she hadn't provided a return address, I had no way of knowing where she was. All I could do was write some letters and hope she would get them.

June 29, Sunday, almost sailing time
Dear Don,

Your letters came to me just the other day - it seems the people at A. Express aren't as prompt and attentive as you.

Yes, I'm quite cured now, thank you. The aftermath, gave me practically no trouble at all - in fact it was one big holiday... eating, sleeping and doting on the service like a gluttonous fish who knows the trick of how to get the worm and not swallow the hook. The reason I draw that simile is because I can't forget what I had for dinner tonite. It was something of the amoebic class smothered in ghostly white yoghurt-consistency sauce. If I had the time, I'd go back to the hospital, but I'm afraid they don't have machines to diagnose this case. Human resistance is at a slow retreat.

When do you start that long mile home? Enjoy the last bit of cool weather - from what I hear, they started the old cuisine trick of cooking omelettes on the sidewalk at home. But it's home and I guess that's the American way.

Was walking down the street yesterday and heard in the background an old western tune slowly being plucked and sung in a familiar sounding drawl. I looked around and saw a small crowd gathered around a blue-jeaned, rather half-starved looking Oklahoman. Seems he and his guitar have been in Paris for several months now, trying to make friends with the cold, unfriendly world. While standing there, I head some Americans talking and it turned out that both were sort of talent-scouting for entertainment at the U.S. pavilion at Brussels. The boy was so convincing that he had signed a contract in 10 minutes. End of today's drama... of no significance but is a good indications of what has happened in Paris once you left - nothing.

Well, here we are... both of us going home and neither of us really sure to what. Our lives are certainly going to change their courses this next month - yours in particular.

Will be anxiously awaiting your next letter - have a happy adjustment, my dear. There won't be anymore "all the old familiar places" like the Eiffel Tower or walks in parks, or policemen at midnight... but to quote Scarlett, "I'll think about that tomorrow."

Love always, Carole

Well, good-bye, Carole. It was nice knowing you. You can think about "tomorrow," but so can I and the next day and the next. This terrific girl was gone, and I had a sinking feeling that there was more to this story than I knew - more unsaid between the lines than on the lines. Or was it my imagination?

For now, though, I had to dig out my one tie, knit, slightly purplish to match the dots in my sport coat, for Christiana and I were going to spend all day Sunday traipsing amongst the *vacationeurs* at *Travemünde*. This was to be a special day and turned out to be more special than I ever dreamed. But not for the usual reasons.

I picked her up in my spiffy soon-to-be-shipped-to-America VW and we headed north to the resort. She was splendidly outfitted in an all-white dress, white gloves, shoes and even had a white ribbon in her hair. Almost like a bride. She looked great! We spent most of the morning ambling along the boat docks, looking into yachts, snapping pictures, and just generally enjoying the ambiance. We had a quick lunch at a brat stand and then headed back to the water for more sightseeing.

All this time and I had never taken a picture of Christiana. She didn't really want to be photographed, but I kept harping and finally I talked her into sitting carefully on the grass. As I snapped the picture, I was overcome by the strangest revelation. It was like "click" and then I knew that she would soon be an "ex," never to be a permanent part of my life. One moment this truly awesome human being that was about as perfect as any female I had ever met and whose gentle personality was perhaps the perfect mate for a gadabout like me went from "number one" or at least "number one and a half" to "I think we should get back now." It caught me by surprise and we silently walked back to the VW and drove back to town mostly in silence.

She asked me what was wrong, but I had no answers. I felt lousy, not sick, but just lousy, and after I dropped her off, I went to my room and flopped on my bed and stared at the ceiling. There weren't any answers up their, either, so I tried to analyze what just happened. Perhaps at that defining moment, which happened at the push of a shutter release, I realized that my fun time was over. Now my number one priority was to get back to college to finish my education. I knew I had no future without one and I certainly had no qualms about how difficult it would be with no GI Bill, scholarship, or much help from my parents. Bringing home a German wife to the semi-poverty of a college student would have been cruel to both of us.

That seemed like too much to have happened in a split second, but maybe it was a compressed idea and I was just rationalizing. Deep down was there still some faint hope of hooking up with Carole? Most likely whatever happened just happened and I would never have a clue. But I kept wondering if I had just tossed away the girl of my dreams because of money - or lack of it? What was wrong with me? Had common sense finally reared its ugly head? Perhaps.

Other guys were taking home wives and seemed more than a little happy about it. I knew a lot of the girls and they were terrific. But it was apparent that everyone had different circumstances to consider. Several days went by and I didn't see her. I came to realize that I was trying to save us both from grief when I finally had to ship out for home. It may have been a cowardly way to handle a delicate problem, but there was no easy way. I wondered how all the other guys had handled such a problem but were too arrogant to ask for help. I finally realized we had to talk and get things settled and somehow come to closure. Even though I still didn't understand everything - anything - that had happened, I knew that at the very least, I owed her an attempt at an explanation. Through mutual friends, we arranged to meet in front of the friendly neighborhood *Kino* a couple nights later. Nine o'clock sharp.

Two nights later, as I was getting ready to drive over, one of the guys, I think it was Wes Roach, slightly bombed, asked me if I could drive him and two girls over to the other house on Zwingli *Strasse*. Bar girls would be a more appropriate term, but I agreed. But then they diddled and dawdled and finally got into the car and we took off. The route to Zwingli took me right past the *Kino* and I knew it was nearing nine o'clock. I realized there was no way I would be on time.

As we sped by the *Kino* a few minutes before nine, I glanced over and there was Christiana, already waiting. She looked back at me speeding by with two laughing semi-drunk bar girls in the car and I knew instantly the look on her face would haunt me forever. Surprise. Astonishment. Heartbreak. Disappointment. Disbelief. Tears. All in a fraction of a second.

I dumped off my passengers and hurried back as fast as I could, but, not surprisingly, she wasn't there. And I didn't blame her. It was purely accidental, but I felt like a totally pathetic human being to cause someone like her that much pain.

I never saw her again, but I knew I would never forget her. I don't know if I deserved the same.

90. Goodby, Christiana

CHAPTER 27: Going, Going, Gone

The last few days of my time in Lübeck I remained a confirmed bachelor. I was now an official "short-timer." I still went to the Riverboat, danced, went to the usual movie parties and witnessed the ongoing minor drunken brawls, but strictly avoided any serious or semi-serious contact with the opposite sex. Because of Christiana, I didn't know if I would ever feel real good about myself again.

91. But I tried: Unknown, Renate, Me, and Kristal

Someone arranged for a softball game in a city park and off we went to perform. We formed teams loosely based on our residence, laid out the bases and got down to business. Of course, there was the usual case or two of good German beer available and I suspect it affected the performance of some. There was also a crowd of natives watching including some kids, and one memorable moment occurred when I fired in a ball from left field and it overshot the catcher and nailed some poor little German kid smack between the eyes. Actually it hit him in the forehead and knocked him off his bike. He dropped like a shot elephant.

Luckily, he must have been a soccer player that was used to headers, but nothing like a hard softball coming in at eighty miles per hour. I was holding my breath as I ran in to check on him, but he bounced right up, gave me a big grin and started rubbing the fast-growing welt on his noodle. He was a tough little guy and stayed around to watch more of this strange game.

Once in a while something extraordinary happens and in this game, I hit what must have been the world's distance record for a softball. I stood and watched the ball rise like a golf ball and disappear out of sight far, far, down the left field line. I slowly began to circle the bases, and the dumb ass acting as umpire screamed "foul ball!" Well, it wasn't, and if it was, he should have had the courtesy to appreciate such a monumental blast. He'd never see one like that again in ten life-times.

92. Bobby Roark at the bat

Before leaving Lübeck, I had to arrange to get my car to Bremerhaven to have all the nasty European germs steam cleaned off and ready for shipment to the Brooklyn Navy Yards. I knew my orders would most likely send me to Fort Hamilton in New York, just a few miles north of the city, to be discharged and sent home. The usual route was from Lübeck, back to

Rothwesten and back to Bremerhaven for a long, slow, stomach-churning boat ride to New York City. I had heard that while waiting in transit at Rothwesten the good old regulars of the ASA made the soon-to-be-ex-soldiers perform all sorts of shit details. Particularly those who came back from the freedom and high-living at Lübeck. I wasn't looking forward to this at all. This was an aspect of army life that kept me from becoming a career soldier. That and my strong love for personal freedom and independence. And true hate of following some dumb shit's stupid orders. Not all the army was like Lübeck.

Fortunately for our national security.

CHAPTER 28: Back at Base Camp Rothwesten

My car was gone, I had no girl friend and mercifully someone back at headquarters in Rothwesten recognized my name and asked if I wouldn't mind coming back a day or two early. There was an important company softball tournament coming up and they needed a pitcher. I replied that I was more of a hitter than a pitcher and that I hadn't pitched for over three years, but if they could live with that, I'd be right down. He sealed the deal when he mentioned that it might be possible to arrange a flight home for me instead of riding on the dreaded USS Butner, the puke special.

So, with a few handshakes and see ya laters, I was gone. Lübeck was history. *Auf Wiedersehen,* Sweetheart. This time, as a true short-timer, I got to ride in the front of the truck. When I reached Rothwesten, I was assigned a bunk on the second floor of a relatively new barracks. Strangely, I was the only person on the whole floor. It was like a private suite. A very large and empty private suite.

The softball tournament was the usual high-importance item on the company commander's agenda, so I was given the royal treatment. I was allowed to sleep as long as I wished, as long as I made the games, go to the mess hall and order whatever I wanted whenever I wanted and for the four or five days I was to be there, given free rein to do whatever I damn well pleased. Who said jocks don't get preferential treatment? Not me.

The tournament was a bust. I didn't know a soul on my team and they didn't know me. After one quick practice, it was apparent to me that I was the best hitter there, but as the pitcher, I was assigned to bat ninth, which meant I would get the least at bats and was just some stupid coaches traditional rule. Pitchers bat last. My pitching left much to be desired, as I suspected it would, but I did manage to hit one home run and a few singles before I was yanked. I didn't stay around to see who won because, as everyone knows, when you're taken out, you hit the showers. That was fine with me. Dumb ass coach. If I couldn't pitch for dick, he should have put me in at another position in order to get the best use of my bat.

160

The next day and the next the games were rained out and the day after I was out of there in a big hurry. Because I stayed longer in Germany for the softball tournament, if I took the slow boat home I wouldn't reach the USA before my enlistment was officially up. Promise made, promise kept. I was assigned to fly out of Frankfurt RheinMain. That was OK with me.

Back in the reassignment barracks in Frankfurt; one more day in Germany. Oh, my God! The Marines have landed in Lebanon and word is out that no one is going home right now. Shivers went through the 30 or 40 of us headed for discharge. There was potential for war in the Middle East, and you don't know what those damn Russians will do. But anyway, get your duffel bags and get on the bus. We're going to the airport.

After a couple hours standing around under the big TWA plane with pins and needles shooting unsympathetically through our bodies, the pilot or someone in authority finally stuck his head out of the door and said, "Get on, someone finally figured out that the army will manage without you." With a whoop we all headed up the ramp. We were on our way!

July 14
Dear Don,

Oh, have you got a surprise waiting for you! The United States looks wonderful.. we had a rough crossing which landed us right in the middle of hot, humid New York. I thought about you many times while being run over by quadruple headlites, triple-tailed, bull-dozer-like cars... just wondering how you and the little tan one are going to survive it all. The mad, speed track world is all coming back to me and the suddenness of it all tends to set you in a little island all by yourself. At times I miss Europe terribly - somehow loneliness there had its compensations. But we can't forget 22 years, and I can forget one - but it'll be hard.

I'm anxious to know what it's gonna' be like for you. Let me warn you of one thing ..No!.. it isn't worth the effort to try to tell anyone, outside of your family, your little experiences and travel stories. I've found it most frustrating, and have ended up with a big "forget it" or else leaving the listener with a completely misinterpreted impression of Europe...this is a warning. (i.e. just try to describe the American pavilion)

Like most children, I have gravely neglected seeing aunts and uncles which are scattered all over the South. Your arrival in Atlanta is about 4 days after I'm supposed to leave with my family on a short vacation. I don't know whether I'll be able to avoid it or not.. if I had been here all this year I would feel free to just tell them that I couldn't go, but Don, it look like I'm going to have to go as much as I'd rather not. If I could have come home when I was supposed to, all of this visiting would be over with. How I wish this sense of obligation would outgrow me, but as long as I'm living under the same roof, etc. etc.

So, where does all this leave us? Despite my wishes, I guess on a correspondence jag...if you're willing? As yet I still don't have a job and am seriously considering the bronco West as an outpost. As you can see my thought processes on my part are temporarily non-functioning - but what's left does tell me I'm going to miss seeing you and wish a meeting possible - all I can ask is that you understand my position and that if you still wish, I want very much to keep writing and maybe possibly plan a real French rende-vous in late summer or late autumn - my wonderlust will definitely be upon me again and as you well know, I accept nothing as impossible,

Have a happy adjustment, my dear.
Love,
Carole

Chapter 29: Being Extraordinary

93. Our view of the TWA flight deck

Although the TWA pilots had spiced up the ride home a bit by letting us peek into the cockpit for a look around at all the dials and gauges, the arrival at New York's La Guardia field was anti-climatic, and I had no feelings, one way or the other, about being back in the good old US of A. I was still in the army. After a short bus ride to Fort Hamilton on the city's outskirts, we were all settled in a barracks, pretty much holding our breath until we knew what was going on while we waited to be officially discharged.

It took a few days to be processed, but here we were, back in the regular army and some of us even got pulled out for KP duty. However, after one day cleaning up someone else's mess, I requested a pass for the day and got on the subway train and rode clear across town to Yankee Stadium to watch a game between the Yanks and the Kansas City Royals. What a thrill that was, to see the monument to Babe Ruth way out there in center field.

I began to think a bit about trying out again for a professional baseball team. A few days before I left for my army tour, I had tried out over a two day period at a camp for the Milwaukee Braves. I was told to come and see them again when I got discharged, and maybe they could work something out, but it was something not high on my agenda. I could hit, throw, and catch a ball with any of them, but I was basically raw, very raw material without any coaching except reading through a book on baseball by Lou Boudreau.

My baseball experience in Lübeck was limited to one afternoon in the garden behind our headquarters mansion at JW *Strasse* 10 when was I playing catch with some of the guys and Marcus Kehrli came out all proud with a brand new catcher's mitt and chest protector and asked me to throw a few hard ones at him. Some fool was brave enough to stand in as a make-believe batter and I carefully threw a couple into Kehrli's mitt. He told me to really, really throw a hard one, as he wanted to see if he could catch it.

I asked the batter to move away, because I didn't trust myself and warned Kehrli to be ready for anything. I cranked up and fired as hard as I possibly could. I will never forget that split second as the ball rocketed straight for Kehrli's round, ruddy, face, positioned right above his glove, and I don't know how he did it, but he seemed to retract his head like a turtle and the ball whizzed through the vacant space where his head had been and ricocheted off the garden wall some 40 feet behind and bounced back to his feet. He picked up the ball, tossed it back to me and wordlessly dropped his new equipment on the ground and walked back into the house.

Presumably to the bar.

I broke out in a cold sweat as I realized that if he hadn't ducked, he would probably have died instantaneously, with a baseball firmly implanted in his forehead. We all laughed about it later - with relief - but that was the last time I ever threw that hard again - at least from a pitcher's distance.

94. The Mighty

95. Pitch

Back in New York, the Babe Ruth's Yankee Stadium spirit must have been catching, for the next evening, I wandered over to the gigantic parade ground in the center of Fort Hamilton and idly watched some kids hitting and shagging fly balls. The spirit moved me to ask if they minded if I hit a few, so I grabbed a bat and the baseball and began to stroke some "fungos" as they say in the trade. I never understood or liked that term, so to me, I was just hitting "flies." Anyway, as I got warmed up I kept hitting them farther and farther and putting more and more effort into it. The last dozen or so must have gone well over 500 feet, almost 1 5/6 football fields, as now it took three of the kids trying in vain to get under one of the towering drives to relay the ball back to me. Mostly, they would just let them hit the ground, for I think they were afraid. They must have thought I was Micky Mantle or something, but I've never seen any baseballs hit farther, especially by just tossing them up in the air and whacking away. It finally ended when I started to tire and the kids got too exhausted to chase any more, and I walked away wondering what the hell just happened?

One evening of being extraordinary happened a few weeks before I was to depart Lübeck. I was looking out the front window as a small, slim, cute girl and her pals wandered past the JW *Strasse* stud farm. For some strange reason, the house was empty and I was sitting in for a few hours as the night orderly for Jim Young, who had to meet his girl friend somewhere. I invited them in to look around. She told her friends to scram and she came boldly up the steps and into the orderly room where Jim had set the radio on a German classical music station. She moved gracefully to the center of the room with the walk and poise of what I imagined a ballet dancer would have. She spoke virtually no English, but began to glide around the room and indicated she wanted me dance with her. So I cranked the radio and began to try to imitate her moves. This was not the typical Riverboat hopping and grinding, but serious, classical dancing, and I didn't have the faintest idea of what was going on. But she led and through her actions showed me what to do. Soon, I was spinning her in pirouettes and actually lifting her in the air overhead and gently turning as she floated back to earth. This was weird stuff for me, really weird, but intensely invigorating, and I thought we were doing a relatively decent job of improvising. All we needed were a pair of tights and a tutu. After about twenty minutes, it was over. She had a happy flush in her face and said she had to be home by nine.

Luckily, just as we just finished dancing, Jim Young came in, gave me a strange look, like, are you robbing the cradle, or what? He took over the orderly room duty so I said I would take her in my car to wherever she had to go. We left quickly with me wondering what the hell just happened? I was glad no one came in while we were dancing for I would have been seriously embarrassed to be seen leaping and doing my best imitation of Rudolf Nureyev. We rode with not much talk, and I drove her to the edge of Lübeck, to someplace I didn't even know existed. It was some sort of a camp and I dropped her off in the center of a collection of tents and ramshackle huts.

I suspected she was a refugee, obviously a dance student at one time, and probably from East Germany or Poland. Although the evening had been strangely and perfectly enjoyable, I also suspected she was way too young to seriously pursue. I wasn't language capable enough to find out what she was doing parading in front of our house, but, again, I speculated she could have been looking for exactly what she got - someone to dance with. I, being the perfect gentleman *ballerino*, bid her good evening. She thanked me profusely for *"tanzen"* and we shook hands and that was the last time I ever saw her. This was truly an extraordinary event that I never discussed with anybody.

CHAPTER 30: Being Unordinary

After I finished my brief physical, collected my last pay, and saluted some Major or something as I received my official discharge papers, I picked up my gear, hopped the subway to Brooklyn Navy Yard and re-established connection with my trusty VW. It had survived the trans-Atlantic crossing without mishap, and everything seemed to work just fine. I filled up with gas and headed west, under the Hudson and down the New Jersey Turnpike. Georgia, here I come; Mom can wait.

It was strange being home; the coffee was universally terrible and the hamburgers wonderful, but at least I could speak the language. Sort of. Driving through the South with a VW wasn't too smart a thing to do, as I found out. Some people apparently thought we were still at war with the Germans and what the hell are you driving a German car over here for? You're an American soldier; you should be driving a car made in America.

I had written Carole that I was going to stop in and see her on my way home and since dipping down through the South wasn't that far out of the way, it would be no trouble at all. She wasn't too enthusiastic in her last letter, but I told her I was coming anyway. No matter what. She was visiting some relatives in Atlanta, so that's where I would go. At least she had the courtesy to give me a phone number to call.

I arrived well after midnight and decided to park my car in some relatively open spot and get some sleep. I found the parking lot outside the Ponce de Leon baseball park - home of the Atlanta Crackers - and fell blissfully asleep. Morning came too soon, so I found a diner for food and peeing and furtively scraping off what stubble I had grown. Carole wasn't there when I called the number she had given me so I told whoever answered the phone that I would be there around ten. I had plenty of time to burn so I slowly made my way down (or up) Peachtree Street to an area in north Atlanta. This was a big, big city, but I had no trouble finding the address. I parked my car in front a huge, low, ranch-style house comfortably hiding behind some big trees and a huge lawn. Really nice.

As soon as I got out of the car, Carole rushed out to greet me with a big hug and said she would like to take me out to lunch at this club her relatives belonged to. Big deal. Strangely, there was no, let's go in the house and meet my uncle. She seemed a little tense, but so was I and that was understandable since we hadn't seen each other for several months. But something just didn't seem right, and I was soon to find out why. The language was different; the food, the traffic, the bigness of the city all made me more than a little uncomfortable. Something was out of place.

It was me. We went to a country club on the outskirts of Atlanta. It had a huge pool, outdoor tables, white-coated black waiters, people happily baking themselves in the noontime sun. Snooty rich people happily baking themselves in the noontime sun. Carole introduced me to some of her friends there, but I could tell I was as welcome as yesterday's french fries. Northerner. Poor dumb small town hick ex-soldier without the proverbial pot to piss in, at that. We ordered lunch, but I found that suddenly I wasn't very hungry and would just as soon get the hell out of there. I felt more at home in Germany; I didn't belong here and frankly didn't want to.

After about an hour of collecting a sunburn, and what passed for polite conversation, we finally drove back to the house in north Atlanta and, once again, I parked in front. Even I could sense that something was bothering Carole. This was not the happy-go-lucky free spirit that I had known in Paris and Brussels. This was not the one who could talk the leaves off a tree about anything and everything; the writer of brilliant, thoughtful letters; the girl who had stolen my heart, at least for a while.

As soon as the car stopped rolling, she took my hands and began to talk, but there were tears in her voice and tears in her eyes. Before she even began to speak, I sensed that this was it - the dreaded brush-off, the inevitable good-by. After the events of the short day, I felt a sense of relief as she verbally and tearfully delivered her "Dear John" letter. She told me that she had ostensibly gone to Paris to go to school, but that it was actually to get over this guy she had been seeing. Meeting me and liking me a whole lot more than she had planned, she thought, would help her get her priorities straight. It sure did!

When she returned home she found that I had stirred some powerful primordial maternal instinct in her, and she discovered that she felt even stronger ties for her former boyfriend. How all this worked was way beyond me. In fact, they were planning on getting engaged shortly. In some twisted way, because of magnificent me, she had found her true love.

Boink! And I had left the sweetest girl in Germany for this. There wasn't much I could say, except that we did have some good memories. As a matter of fact, some unusual once-in-a-life-time memories. I wished her - and lucky him - well and inanely, struggling for something to say, hoped that someday I could have a house as nice as this one. She gave me a quick peck on the cheek and with a I'll never forget you and let's keep in touch, she fled across the grass. That was that.

I was a free man, but I didn't know if that was good or bad.

96. Back to earth

Notes and Anecdotes from Other Lübeckers

CHAPTER 31: Courtesy *The Lübeck Association Newsletter;* Tales From the Internet, and, Particularly, Selected Confessions From Dave Savignac's Book, *The Lübeckers.*

In a note from the "other side," **Christa Maria Hahn** tells about her feelings about the invaders, the dreaded "Ami's."

Love Conquers All (or how I was able to love the Ami's and accept Thanksgiving)

I grew up in the house on the corner of Luther and Zwingli Strasses, and when I was a teenager, I absolutely detested the presence of the Ami's. The main reason was because they had loud cars, which always needed shifting at my corner, talked loud, wore those white socks and T-shirts, all the while chewing gum. I had no confidence in them ever defending my little old Lübeck. They played some kind of "ball" in the street, again loud, and my nose was somewhat rumpled when I saw them. Never mind the girls from the neighborhood who dated them, surely it wasn't going to be me.

One event I will never get out of my head. My friend Chrischi's dog was about to give up her puppies and needed a bed. So we went to my house and used my stuffed animals to make a dog bed, and take it back to her house. About at the corner, as we were giggling, walking with this dog bed between us, a U.S. Army truck comes careening around the corner with a soldier playing the piano in the back of the truck. Here we were two teenagers who thought they looked funny totally frozen with our mouths open..... I've always wondered who that piano player was

I must say I still had my nose in the air somewhat about the Ami's until 1963. That's when my friends Heide, Elke, and Silka encouraged me to find out more about the U.S. and to experience a "real" Thanksgiving. At that time, my friends were already in the States, but somehow, I can't remember how I got connected to a Phil Schwartz, who was to take me to the billets in Blankensee for the famous feast.

Of course, the whole occasion was overshadowed by the death of President Kennedy. I was to be picked up at the Post Office, and waited for what seemed like hours, in the snowfall, for my ride....I must say my opinions about the Ami's had not improved.

The dinner was a huge disappointment, rubber turkey, watery broccoli and some goo that was supposed to be the famous pumpkin pie.

My feeling was to get out of there as fast as I could, but I was stuck. There was no bus available, so I had to wait for someone to give me a ride. Most of the boys went on to a poker game and left me to stew in boredom, but one man caught my eye. He volunteered to vie me a ride home.....that man was Ed Hahn. He sort of changed my idea about the "unmannered" and "uncivilized" Ami's

We were married a year later on Thanksgiving day, with another Thanksgiving dinner that was much better, having been prepared by a regular chef at Ed's instructions.

The rest is history.....

Christa-Maria tells why we were never allowed to go to Berlin. Apparently we were all famous and didn't know about it!

When I met Bill, I had no idea why or what American's were doing in my town, neither did I want to know much. Always thought the least I knew the better off I would be. When Bill and I were engaged, I went for a graduation trip with my bank class to Berlin via bus. At the border crossing from West Berlin to East Berlin, they took our ID's asked how much money we had and let us sit and sweat.

Then the guard came back and pulled a few of us from the bus. Two guys who had been in the German army and me.
Why me?

They knew I was engaged to Bill, even knew his serial number, and proceeded to tell me what he was doing*. I had no clue until then. It was scary to sit there and to be interrogated, but they must have felt I really knew nothing and let me go. They told me Bill was on "abhör Geräten" (listening devices). But I did not know that he spoke Russian until we were married. We*

had a little apartment on Eschenburgstrasse; the back had
balconies overlooking the harbor. Around Christmas time, we
had a little tree outside on the balcony and one crisp day, I saw
him standing there intently listening to some people speaking to
each other in a foreign language. He said it was Russian.

Bill's German was very good, he could understand about
everything, but was slow to speak, which drove my family crazy.
They thought it was rather impolite, but he was afraid to have
Russian words come out by mistake.

Christa-Maria reminiscing about her family in Lübeck:

Being German born in 1944, I thank those courageous men
and women who fought to liberate us from Hitler from my heart.
Being rather outspoken I would not have had a chance under him
and any system that has masses following like sheep is not my
cup of tea.

My father fought in WW2, in France, Belgium, and Holland.
He was a clerk and never talked about the war, neither did
anyone else. Neither did anyone ask questions. He died when I
was 24. Ten years ago, after my stepmother's death, I got a metal
box with some special things' in it. It contained my father's
ribbons and medals, iron crosses and also a letter from his
business trying to keep him from the war draft. My father
worked in the iron and steel business, they thought he would
have been more useful staying home.

This box also solved a mystery to me; at about that 4 years
old, people came into my house and took all of our furniture. For
a 4 year old that was rather traumatic, for I remember it clearly
to this day. And no one gave me an explanation, which was the
part I puzzled over for many years, but than "good German little
girls" do not ask questions.

In my father's metal box was a letter (receipt) about this
furniture from the British occupation, to be sent back to Holland.
Since my father is dead, and so is everyone else that could
remember, I must assume our furniture was war booty...but it has
made me wonder: was he a clerk that kicked Jews out of their
houses? No one in my family ever showed any dislike for Jewish
people or talked about "that" part of the war.

My uncle, who was 15 at that time, made friends with an occupation soldier named, Ted. Several years ago, my aunt, who gives tours in Lübeck, was asked by a British couple, if they knew a Reinhold Schoen. That was my uncle and the person asking was Ted. My uncle, Reinhold, had died years before, but my aunt gave him the tour of the rebuilt business houses next to the Clemenstrasse; "Max Schoen, Eisen and Sanitär", on the Untertrave.

I got in touch with Ted via internet, for he had pictures for me. He told me, that the night he had his goodby party, my father came home after having been a POW for two years by the American's on the Rhine River. First my father was shocked to find soldiers in our house. Then he joined in the party.

Ted also sent me a picture of my mother in an Airforce uniform, she did some telephone work. I had no idea...

Although my father never spoke an unfriendly word about Americans, he was not happy about me marrying Ed Hahn. He disowned me on my wedding day via a registered letter. Ed never met him.

I don't know about the other girls that married GI's but for my family it was a shock and not welcomed. To this day, I am the black sheep, the deserter. But then I came from a family much like Thomas Mann wrote about in the *Buddenbrooks*, an old Lübecker patrician Hanseatic family.

I miss the history of Lübeck, miss the gothic sturdiness, the feeling of "it always has been so" at times. Never mind the marzipan and good bread. But my life in the US, despite some large hurdles has turned out OK. I live close to Lake Michigan , which is not the Baltic, but it's water.

97. Yes, Lübeck harbor was deep enough and big enough for ships

From the earliest establishment of the Lübeck detachment, those who preceded me set the grand tone for the fabulous Lübecker decadent lifestyle of the not so rich and, because of the secrecy issue, not so famous. Not all the players, however, were of the wild and woolly type. At least in their letters home.

John Hills: from the early days of the Lübeck detachment
Nov. 3, 1954. Fortune's wheel has turned and the ASA at last is paying off! This morning nine of us left our detachment at Bahrdorf and tonight we are ensconced in what looks like a consulate or fraternity house in the best neighborhood of Lübeck, 45 miles north of Hamburg, almost on the Baltic. We will be doing the same work as we have done all summer, but now we live in comfort, and eat all our meals at a gasthaus near where we work. We live in the city and drive out 7 or 8 miles into the country to work and eat. We will be receiving per diem pay to cover meals, maid service, etc. Our stay is indefinite, depending on how successful operations are this month and next. If we have success, we may stay here for the winter and coming spring and summer.

175

Nov. 9, 1954. I haven't seen TV over here, except for that rural gasthaus near Kassel last April, when we were on our first Spring Patrol. There are American Forces radio stations here, but the only TV is German and not very interesting.... An inspection team (Major, Captain, and lesser flunkies) is expected tomorrow, so everyone, soldiers, maids, and two house painters, has been busy getting our own things and the house and yard ready! The rear yard recently was messed up by the removal of a couple of trees, so there was much raking and work to do. The yard runs down to the water (not a river, but an arm of the river-canal-harbor system, which encircles Lübeck 17 km. up the River Trave from the sea) Beyond the water are boating houses, old roofs and chimneys, and the spires and towers of the city - quite an unusual picture. Lübeck reminds me of Portsmouth, New Hampshire or Salem, Massachusetts - old, aristocratic, brick, somewhat fallen on poor times. There are a lot of good shops in the city and picturesque streets and marketplaces for good-weather trips (we have had several wet days).

Saturday night we heard "La Traviata" - Violetta was excellent, Alfredo terrible (voice and stage manner), Alfredo's father good and the chorus made up of hags and old men. It was staged with gaslights and bustles - I had thought it crinolines circa 1860. The scenery was terribly huge and heavy - Violetta's villa looked like the somber sepulchral chapel that Michelangelo built for the Medici's in Florence!

Nov. 16, 1954. I picked up this card, a colored photo of Lübeck, at a bookstore - it may give you some idea of the city. The tipsy towers in the foreground are those of the Holstentor, formerly the main gate of the old city walls. It now houses material related to the history of Lübeck and the Hanseatic League. The little towers behind the gate are those of the Rathaus, bombed and now rebuilt. The large church is the Marienkirche - badly bombed and now still a sad sight. It's steeples burned in the big air raid of 1942.

Bob Edsall and I had a marvelous time last Sunday, exploring the city. It was a fine, clear, brisk November day, especially pleasant along the canals and river. The city is ringed by water - the Trave River on the south and west and the Trave-Elbe in the north and east. The Cathedral (also badly bombed) lies in the eastern end of town, above old millponds, which now form a beautiful lake, filled with seagulls and a few swans. In the evening, we went to a concert of Abendmusik in the cathedral (organ, organ and violin, and choral pieces. The lighting was from candles in a huge hanging brass chandelier.

Nov. 22, 1954... Although we live in a private house in a residential section of Lübeck, it is obvious to the Germans that we are in the U.S. Army, for we wear uniforms to work (and if we go downtown in the evening), and ride around in Army trucks or cars with U.S. Forces in Germany plates. The British intelligence men who live next door have repeatedly suggested to our officers that we wear noting but civilian clothing and use civilian vehicles, but we apparently are not to be trusted out of uniform in this immediate vicinity.

Nov. 29, 1954. On Thanksgiving Day we actually had a turkey and pumpkin pie: Mutti (Frau Else Kruger, the proprietress of the restaurant Fliegerhorst, where we eat) roasted a bird, and made some good whip cream topped pumpkin pies, and as she always does, went all out to give us a good meal and a semblance of a Thanksgiving dinner. The officer of this detachment, who has been with us for a week to shape us up for a big inspection in December, stood us all to wine... My German remains pretty small, but is enough to stand me in stead in railways, hotels, stores, and restaurants. I think all those months of studying Russian have queered me on making an intensive study of German. We use a little Russian in our work, but do not speak it much in the house, and not at all outside, unless we go to the Russian restaurant in Hamburg.

Dec. 12, 1954. Four of us went to Mozart's "Abduction from the Seraglio" last night. It was a new presentation and it seems as if we should have waited several weeks until the singers were familiar with the music. I am just about through with going to the Lübeck opera - how I long for a good American musical. We are on break beginning tonight, so tomorrow I am going to Hamburg to read in the Amerikahaus and perhaps see a movie in an English theater.

Dec. 15. I am at work now (6:30 p.m.) after spending the morning preparing for another fool inspection. We had one two weeks ago - this was an exact repeat - and both were to shape us

up for the big inspection between Christmas and New Year's.
Last time my tent poles and shovel were fine - this time
(untouched) they need repainting. This is the stupid way it goes.
I am utterly sick of all this evaluation by appearances and mad
erecting of Potemkin villages" every time and officer or
inspection draws near. Well, just over six months to go!...On
payday last we were not paid our per diem, so we had to pay
restaurant and house bills (maid, coffee, spam, eggs, and bread
for snacks) out of our own monthly pay. It will be a penurious
Christmas and New Year's for most of us! But the next payday
should turn us into Rockefellers!

Jan. 2, 1955. We are driving back to Giessen this Tuesday -
the ten of us will go in two private cars, the baggage will go by
truck. We are sitting in the small living room now - the rest of
the house is cold, as the furnace fire went out last night and was
only started again after tonight's supper. The pay officer got
here this afternoon. Everybody had large bills at Mutti's - meals,
maid, and Christmas spirits.... New Year's Eve was as unusual as
was Christmas Eve (which included a lively party at Jürgen-
Wullenwever #10, with dancing, etc. and the local ladies
pursuing GI's into the attic). When the midnight shift got out to
the Site, the horizon was lit with flashes from fireworks, making
the sky over Lübeck very brilliant.

Finally, at the very end, it appears from John's letters that
there was more stuff going on in the little detachment than the
local opera. It would be nice to see his letters to someone other
than his parents. The Lübecker tradition seems to have been in
full swing in early 1955. But like John, not everyone was playing
to the same drummer. Another John, John Dinwiddie, arrived
about five years later.

John Dinwiddie:
My own experience was somewhat private. I met a woman
early on, to whom I have been married ever since. We kept to
ourselves for the most part. I came to Lübeck at a time when an
old guard was being phased out and was for its own reasons
pretty resentful of newks. I was 20 years old, eccentric even by
Lübeck standards, and took a lot of hazing as a result.

178

I responded by inventing my own Lübeck, something that in one way or another every newk not a part of the Janicki empire had to do. My own version amounted to learning - and not easily - the ins and outs of a German family coping with the threat of an American intent on marrying one of theirs....

Gerda and I never had a car, biked, bussed or trained to every part of Schleswig Holstein we could get to, taking hundreds of photos of everything, especially the reconstruction of the war damaged brick-Gothic monuments. I stayed after discharge and studied at the music conservatory in Hamburg....

More from an "older and even wiser" **John Dinwiddie** from Dave Savignac's "The Lübeckers," written in the late 90's.

"I like Lübeckers; we're older and wiser and still reasonably smart. Let's party. But the old Lübeck was not the monolithic myth that defined a universe crammed between the Riverboat and Clemenstrasse, though one at least was certainly a virtuous affair; some of the greatest jazz I ever heard transpired at the Riverboat, still there, semi-abandoned. The Lübeck beyond was one of the most astounding concentrations of culture in Europe, still is, although sadly, no more opera. No more symphony. Christoph Dohnanyi, son of the Hungarian composer, nephew of a celebrated anti-Nazi partisan, was conductor. Now he leads one of the best orchestras in the world. Von Weber, who had been director of Brecht's theater in Berlin, now did Brecht in Lübeck,

A couple of weeks ago Gerda and I went to a performance of Mozart's strangely second rate Requiem - his fault, not Sussmayr's . But this stentorian neo-Baroque affair sure does its thing when attached to a Gothic cathedral instead of a county veterans' administration building.

When I was a part time student at the Schleswig-Holsteinische Musikakademie und Nordeutsche Orgelschüle (no kidding) right in Lübeck in two mansions a half klick up Travemünde Allee from the Burgtor, we did this old turkey in the Jacobi Kirche, and with my adolescent tastes I thought I'd gone to heaven. A big chord stop and we in the chorus loft almost see it cross the nave, ricochet off the cloister, and come back to greet us sometime later, usually before the next piece.

So when Gerda heard our first big one, the Mozart C Minor which would have made Bach jealous, in the Dom, well, I left the building a different man.

I once was let into the catwalks above the domes of Marienkirche. On top they looked like bee hives. Consider the problem of imitating stone Gothic with brick, but anyone doing so must maintain a state of denial which falls short of looking down from a dome almost two hundred feet above the floor whose keystone is one little pancake of a brick. It was a slice.

When the church was bombed every one of them went, leaving the flying buttresses to lean against virtually nothing but vertical wall and what was left of the ribbing. Then it began to rain - and this was Palm Sunday, 1942. Marien was about to implode and collapse altogether. Gerda, born in 1941, spent that night with her family in her basement coal bin. She has written a book about extensions of this subject, has yet to finish it. So the Red Cross moved refugees into the city in order to prevent Bomber Harris from coming back to finish the job, and the Germans commandeered all the bootleg canvas they could find, fashioned a shroud which covered the corpse, as it were, until in 1947 when Thomas Mann raised funds to restore it. Gerda remembers the date confronting Mann's effort - people were still starving here and there. Gerda watched the reconstruction from her schoolroom window.

Which brings us to the 60's. When I was escaping the mercies of the Janicki gang, I wandered about the town with my camera, and one fine day at the Dom I went through the fence, keeping all but the ghosts out of the totally destroyed cloisters area, a magnificent Gothic addendum to this Romanesque beast which Doug Card once dismissed as a barn - but what a barn! Signs with the usual temptations - Lebensgefahr, Eintritt Verboten, all that good stuff. In I went.

The sun in the west lit the compass of ruined colonnades like a theater stage. On the ground grass had grown around the ancient limestone gravesheets that made up the floor. Many of them were shattered as if their occupants had exploded through them. Looking up, all of the main columns had survived and much of the ribbing for the domes outlined the devastation. Small bushes grew on top of these ribs, having found

*nourishment in the bricks over the years of exposure. One of the
columns had a circular staircase in it, which I climbed. Three
quarters of the way up, the outer wall had failed so that the
stairwell looked like a brickwork screw when seen from below.
That's how I realized that it was there. It was a de Chirico
landscape. ..."*

98. Fallen bells from air raid, *Marienkirche*; photo by M. Havis

Bob Fleming,

*There was a German glider club that had a hanger on the
airfield. We were always amazed at how high they could go in
the gliders. They were ex-Luftwaffe for the most part. They
weren't allowed to have propeller-driven planes when we first
got there. In May of either 1955 or 56 the Germans regained
their sovereignty and suddenly the glider had a propeller-driven
plane that came out of nowhere. They had their monthly
meetings at Mutti's and seemed to be pretty nice guys.*

*Adjacent to the airfield on the side opposite Mutti's was
where the German Border Guard Academy was located. They
had a few of us over one night for a few beers. It became obvious
that these guys were ex-German Army soldaten. Unfortunately,
as a result of a beer-driven discussion things became a little
tense. Fortunately nothing physical. We were never invited*

back, and we never invited them to our place. As a matter of fact, I can't recall ever seeing any of them except on their barrack grounds. Germany didn't have an army, so the Border Guard Academy was the West Point of the Border Guards.

99. Two graduates of BGA (Duain Shaw photo)

Charlie Metz:

Another story I heard about. After two or three years when the Headquarters finally located Lübeck on the map, and after we survived the onslaught of the "Visitors," the powers that be decided that we needed some spiritual guidance, and sent what I call "circuit rider priests" around to all the detachments within the command.

One such priest arrived at Lübeck - he was a big man, and some said that he was from Holland. In an attempt to round up his flock for Sunday services, he agreed to go downtown with them for a beer if they would agree to attend church services on Sunday. Those poor misguided fools - little did they know that they had just made a pact with the Devil himself. Not only did he go to town with them - he proceeded to drink most of them under the table. But he did help get all the men home safe and sound.

182

*As promised, the Father went around to their rooms at about
6:00 a.m. to roust them out to attend services. After much
groaning and complaining, and promises of resurrections, and
assurance that there is life after death, they all finally assembled
for services. The subject of the sermon was - you guessed it -
Moderation!*

*After regular services, he conducted confessional services
for the Catholic members. When last observed, he was still
praying to the Big Fellow up above trying to work out a deal to
absolve them of their sins. I think the only answer he ever got
was, "FAT CHANCE!" - for their sins they must apply in person.*

Gene Ellis:

*I moved to Blankensee when the new barracks first opened,
but in accord with typical government planning, it was soon
overcrowded. E-5's were told they could move out and find their
own space while the Army located housing. I lived in the
Reuterkrug Hotel for a while before getting a temporary room on
the Clemenstrasse above a bar and service center (the bartender
was a friend of mine). This bar was always full of Polish sailors
who either wanted to buy me drinks or beat the crap out of me
every time I entered or left my residence.*

*A little later, the Army found me housing. This was a three
bedroom house on the city lake. The owner was a German
contractor who reserved the front room to service his mistresses.
On the few occasions he showed up without his frauleins, he
would buy the Asbach and tell outlandish but very interesting
stories.*

Dave Savignac:

*I got to Lübeck by pure luck. I had spent the previous year at
Sinop-by-the-Sea (Turkey) where I had heard of the wild goings-
on at this little site on the Baltic. I reported to the I.G. Farben
building in Frankfurt for further assignment. They asked (!) me
where I would like to go, and of course, I said Lübeck....*

*They told me that they would fly me to Lübeck by helicopter.
Every morning I would report to see whether the chopper was
scheduled to fly. It was winter, and foggy and, after about a
week, they said, "Grab your gear - we're leaving in fifteen."*

It was a great trip, especially looking down (literally) on the "animal outfits" doing winter training in the snow, thanking God I was in Chairborne. When we arrived someone in the crew said, "Here we are, Mt. Meissner," and two or three people got off. When I said that I was going to Lübeck, they got pissed. "We never fly to Lübeck any more."

On the following day, I was told that the First Shirt, Harlin Hanson, was going to take me to Lübeck in his personal vehicle. I tried to make conversation on the way up, but he didn't say much. I wondered why....

The next morning I learned that there definitely was something about me that the First Shirt didn't like. It was the mustache that remained after I had shaved my beard in Frankfurt. After breakfast that morning, someone - I think it was Bernie McCollum - came up to me and said that Hanson had been swearing at me under his breath for the entire meal! Seems he just didn't like mustaches on soldiers. Of course, Bernie said, I was absolutely within my rights to have mustache if I kept it perfectly trimmed, but he just thought that it wouldn't hurt me to know the First Shirt's feelings on the subject.

I shaved it off that morning before I sent out to the site.

Jon Hunter:

Roy Clark and I were looking for beer on C street as it was closing. A beer truck was making a delivery, but he refused to sell us a beer or two, so when he went into one of the houses we stuck a bunch of marks on the truck seat and took a case of beer. He yelled he was calling the Polizei so we said to hell with him and took the whole truck. We didn't get very far before the police went by. We abandoned the truck and tried to run with beer bottles stuck in every pocket. They kept falling out and left and easy trail for the police to follow.

While in jail Roy came up with an escape plan but because he was the only black in Lübeck, we decided I should be the escapee. It worked and I fled the jail and hid out at Muttis until I finally gave up after several days of being AWOL.

Then it was house arrest at the Z House. After a couple escapes from here they sent me to Kassel to be court-marshaled. Roy got busted but they goofed on me. I got away with orders to

*come home and after one large going away party in the bahnhof
in Hamburg, someone put me on the train to Bremerhaven to
catch my ship. I vaguely remember someone taking me off the
train and putting me in a bunk on the ship. I woke up two days
out to sea. What a trip.*

Harry "Good Back" Walthall:

*In early November, I arrived in Lübeck. I don't remember
how I got there. Mainly I don't remember because I had taken a
liking to booze of almost any flavor or taste...*

*Anyone remember when most of us went on a Pernod kick
that lasted about three or four months? II had bought a BMW
and I recall during the Pernod period waking up with a female
companion telling me that we had unknowingly strayed over the
border. This happened on at least two occasions. I believe that
this was also the time that I was going with the Lübeck's Police
Chief's daughter, Anne, who later married a guy from Company
B. But I could be wrong, because it doesn't seem like that female
companion I mentioned was Anne. In fact, I think it was a
different companion on both occasions.*

*Speaking of Anne and her Police Chief father - this guy
thought I could do no wrong. He and I were close drinking
buddies. He had an orchard in his back yard from which he
made every flavor of schnapps you can think of.*

*There were many Lübecker friends who benefited from my
close friendship with this man, but I won't name names or tell
tales. We made a pact early in our friendship that he would call
me when any of my buddies ran afoul of the law - instead of
notifying the CO and getting them in trouble. Needless to say, I
received many calls from the old boy and was able to help quite
a few fellow Lübeckers without the military finding out.*

Some six months later:

*I arrived in Lübeck about 2:00 AM on Breitestrasse in front
of Ilse (Grim) Campbell's apartment. As soon as I was in her
apartment she excitedly began telling me that my ex-girlfriend,
Anne the Police Chief's daughter, was getting married the
following day to one of the men from Company B. She said that
as the loser, I was supposed to show up at the wedding with
thirteen beautiful roses and give them to Anne.*

So, next day, I go buy thirteen beautiful roses which I take, not to the wedding, but to the reception at her parent's house. Someone answered my doorbell ring and bade me enter, which I did. I had taken about three steps into the room when Anne's old man spotted me. He gave out a shriek, bounded across the room knockingl people in different directions and yelling, "Heinie!" grabbed me in a bear hug and I almost dropped the roses!

I could tell that he was hours past passing any sobriety test. I could also tell that he was not exactly happy about his daughter's marriage. But I played the loser, gave the roses to Anne, and along with aunts, uncles, cousins, Anne's younger brother, etc. celebrated the wedding.

At some point in the celebration, Anne and the groom stand and make the announcement that they are leaving. Leaving for where, you ask? My thoughts exactly, but only briefly, as they announce that they are going to Anne's bedroom. Strange, I think, but the party continued on.

About forty-five minutes after the couple's departure, Anne appears in her nightgown (what a beautiful bride!) and asks, "Has anyone seen the groom?" Several relatives say they haven't. Anne approaches her brother and asks him to go look for the groom. I will not repeat what he said because it was quite negative and very unfriendly to his sister-bride on her wedding night. Feeling quite sorry for Anne, I say that I'll go look for him.

I quite naturally was drawn to the back yard, first because I noticed that the old man was missing, and once I stepped outside I could hear that there was someone out in the fruit orchard. I approached the noise to find the groom with the collar of his pajama's hooked on to the end of a short sawed-off tree branch, legs just a-kickin'. My first thought was, "How'd the old man get him up there?" The old man wasn't being too kind to both sides of the grooms' face, and the groom couldn't do anything about it. So I put the old man in a bear hug from his rear and attempted to calm him down. I was able to move him a few feet from the tree and others in the party were able to get the groom down.

I spent the rest of my time at the party helping to get the old man to bed. I did spend a while with the younger brother in his room. Most of the guests had left. He and I downed a bottle we had taken to the room. I have never returned to Lübeck.

Jack Weber:

Yet another train trip was in store, this time from Heilbronn to Kassel. One day there in processing, then off we went, by 3/4 ton truck (how revolting!) to the land of my soon-to-be-dreams, driven by the 319th Company B motor pool gang - PFC L.L. Laughlin and Sergeant Keller. The trip was the worst experience in my then brilliant military career. We made record tracks, speeding due north from Kassel. Away we flew to our new duty station on the Trave. Looking out from the back of that old truck in the winter cold, I swear my then young life was flashing before my very eyes. My companion, PFC Totman "himself," was laying there hung-over and looking very much like a dead "Mauschen."

The site of our lieber neuer Heimat was breathtaking, to say the least. Yes, I thought that I had finally died and gone to heaven. Arriving at night, we went directly to the ever notorious Zwinglistrasse House. This was to be my home away from home. (Later, they would move me to the Jerk House when it was easier to keep me under surveillance. I roomed there with Dooley Johnson until the end.) I dropped onto the first bunk, fully clothed, and quickly fell off into dreamland.

Charlie Metz:

Kurt, the ex-Lufthansa pilot from pre-WWII days who had the old World War I biplane that he had restored and delighted in buzzing the operations vans out at the airport (while flying upside down). He got a little close one time and clipped the whip antenna on the radio van. Maybe Scott Messenger will remember, because I think he was one of the several who jumped out of the van when they thought he was going to hit. At the time they didn't know that Kurt gave flying demonstrations at air shows, and his forte was flying upside-down and plucking a scarf from the runway. He was a true "Junker."

Another time a bunch of guys were sitting around Jerk House when someone announced that some Belgian pilots were due to arrive at the airport, and it was decided that they should be well and truly greeted Lübeck style. I don't know who all was in the reception committee that went to the airport to await their arrival, but after a while these planes circled and landed, two

*Spitfires and a Seahawk, all of British origin. After they taxied in
and shut down the engines, the welcoming committee rushed to
the planes and forced the pilots to drink a toast with them before
they could get out of the planes. One toast led to another, and I
think they stopped because all the booze was gone.*

*These Belgian pilots were good sports and got their revenge
in kind a few days later. They invited their reception committee
out to Mutti's for a little social get-together and introduced them
to a little Belgian drinkfest ritual; that's where you pair up and
face each other with full glasses of beer. As you take a drink of
beer, you slap your drinking partner lightly on the face; after
each sip of beer the force of the slaps are progressively harder.
There sure were a lot of puffed-up and sore faces the next day.*

Hugh Goodheart:

*Lübeck was a sleepy, medieval town; even the after-hours
bars at the houses of prostitution seemed to come from another
age. I hung out at the Riverboat, mostly because of Annie Arnt,
who tended bar there, and of couple of places along the canal.*

*As an American Jew, I felt uncomfortable most of the time,
but I think the Germans felt uncomfortable around Americans,
too. Every man I met in Germany of an age to fight during the
War was either captured during the first few days of hostilities
or fought on the Eastern Front.*

*On the Jewish High Holidays I went to the synagogue in
town, stripped during the war but left standing because it is right
next to the Marienskirche (stripped during the Reformation). I
felt uncomfortable there, too: diamond merchants from Hamburg
were unfolding handkerchiefs to show each other their wares
during the services! I couldn't follow the Hebrew well, and I
heard one of them tell his young son that all Americans were
stupid like that one. I understood his German perfectly. My best
German friends were fundamentalist Christians....*

*There were eight ex-seminarians at one point in Lübeck; a
couple were within months of ordinations as priests when they
left. I remember Ed Roveto best. He would get tired from
drinking, sometimes, and he would try to lie down on the bar
stool. It never worked, but he kept trying. He would make sad
"baloo" sounds, like an old elephant.*

I knew Maren Huvald in Lübeck - as a friend. I think she was still pining for Davey Wrench, who had left not too long before I arrived. I was told that Davey's great talent was going up on the bridge over the canal and barfing on the swans, but this may be just the malicious slander they tell new guys about the departed.

(Dave Wrench's comment: "I remember jumping from the bridge onto the swans, but barfing, well, I probably did that too).

My two years in Germany changed me, although it's hard to explain exactly how. I had dropped out of college, where I was struggling and moody, to enlist. When I returned I was focused. My friends since then have been very different from me, rather than similar - different in background, profession, even interests. I think maybe I learned how to get past surface differences and to discover similar views about life during that time.

Dog stories from the Hulk and Goodback Harry:

Schatzie was a beauty, I remember her well. She was either a German Shephard or Belgian Malenois. She, along with Becks, Sport, Horrass, Horace DeBussey Jones,and a pup named Ajax made up the nucleus of the dog corps of the Fighting "69-ers," as we were called.

… A young newlywed German couple checked into our Hotel. So, in the restaurant, we warned them that Herr Gromann would lock the front door of the hotel about 11:00 PM, so if they found themselves locked out to come around to the back of the hotel and the kitchen door would be unlocked. One morning around 2:00 AM there was a big commotion in the kitchen. Wes bounded down the stairs into the kitchen to find the young bride, standing on top of the big iron cook stove, with her clothing ensemble in shreds, trying to cover her naked body. Her hubby was lying on the floor still gallantly trying to get Horraas the boxer to release the death grip on his arm.

…Another time Paul Arrowhood was throwing rocks for the pups to fetch. Once, he faked throwing the rock and the pups took off down the concrete runway. Horrass, who was watching peacefully beside the ops hut, didn't hear the rock hit the cement, so he got up and slowly walked over to Paul and, calmly, without warning or growling, bit him in the ankle.

Eulogy by former Lübecker's son, Bowman Gray IV.

Bowman Gray III
Lübeck 1958 - 1960
Russian Linguist

It just happened to arrive on my 32nd birthday - June 13, 2001 - the email out of the blue to my Uncle Lyons Gray from Jack "Hulk" Weber. This was more than serendipitous as I had just gone through the stack of pictures of my dad in Lübeck and Monterey that had been sent to me shortly after my father's passing in 1985. I had had never been told, or at least in the confusion had not heard, who had sent the most candid of shots of my father having what appeared to be a great time. Convertibles, girls, beer and smiles that was the genre of the times and the pictures. These had been very healing gifts from Jack to me sixteen years ago.

After connecting with my new Uncle Hulk, who overwhelmed me with wonderful remembrances of my dad, I began to discover that the apple had not fallen very far from the tree. That summer I began to see my father in a whole new, albeit more human, light. I began to ask my Uncle Lyons questions about my dad in his youth which helped me to understand more about who my father was. This also inspired a much closer relationship with my uncle for which I am grateful and of which I am sure my father would be pleased. Thanks Jack. I wasn't long before I was planning a trip to attend my first Lübecker reunion.

November 2001, Palm Desert, California - what a trip. As I checked in to the hotel I was met by Dick Gauthier with a hand shake that reached back a generation. It was all I could do to keep myself together and judging by Dick's grip and eyes it seemed we both looked at one another looking to catch a glimpse of my dad. The short trip was full of meeting those of you who really knew my dad and reaffirmed the notion that I had not spent my youth entirely too differently than he had. I heard stories of long nights, despised COs, German girlfriends and cars. What I can't offer in my father's memories I can offer in his thanks to all of those he served with. The thanks are for allowing him to be who he was. Without going into great detail, he always

*felt a certain amount of pressure to conform to a family ideal
that did not allow for the personal freedom that he found with his
friends in the Army.*

*Although I have never been to Lübeck or served in the armed
forces, I am grateful for them and the impact that they had on my
dad and subsequently me. Because of his relationships with you,
I now know him better and I have been drawn closer to my own
family. I am honored to be a part of this unique group.*

In addition, Bo writes: following is the write up I did last
year for my dad's bio on the Lübeck web site:

*My father served in the U.S. Army from 1957-1960 the last
year of which he spent as part of the motor pool* (actually, Bo, he
was a 988 Russian Voice Interceptor) *in Lübeck. While on this
journey he was introduced to several well-cultured individuals at
the language school in Monterey. One of whom still impacts our
family to this day - I, of course, speak of the Incredible Hulk who
was singled out by my grandfather to watch out for my dad.
Basically he was made an offer he could not refuse. Everyone
seems to have come away from the experience relatively
unscathed. There are several great friendships that he
remembered to my mother over the years. He was relatively
reserved in speaking of his Lübeck memories to my sisters and
me as he had a fatherly image that he needed to maintain.
Fortunately after spending a little time with Cool Breeze and
having been a part of the 2001 reunion, I now have a more
complete picture drawn of the dens of iniquity that were Zwingli
and Jergen Haus. Having met The Hulk, Dick & Geri and the
rest of the crew in the Desert, I can rest assured knowing that
dad had a blast!*

*I truly believe that he would be pleased to know that not only
do you all remember him well, but that you all have reached out
to his family. The bond that exists between the Lübeckers is more
than that of a fraternity; it is something quite unique and
wonderful. We are honored to be a part of something that meant
so much to my dad.*

100. Zwingli 8 in 2001

101. Canal across the *Wakenitz*

CHAPTER 32: Closing Down is Such a Hard Thing To Do

Eventually, the happy-go-lucky atmosphere of Lübeck station was curtailed somewhat due to the Army building barracks-type structures near the site at *Blankensee*. This had to hurt.

Jim Miller:

The summer of 1961 was very sad, due to the move to Blankensee. Yes, we all had to leave our beloved rooms at Zwingli and Jerk Haus. Nevermore would there be the bar where you could drink for almost nothing, no more could we spy on the girls next door from the attic at Zwingli, or watch Opa cut the grass with a sickle. This was a very dark day in the history of Company B. I think from that day forward Lübeck was changed forever and lost much of its charm. This is not to say that we didn't love and enjoy our stay, but for me it was never quite the same. It was about this time that the "Berlin Crisis" reared its ugly head. We all had our rotation dates extended, for as much as nine months for the short timers to three months for me. Another bummer to be sure... but think about guys in other locations: at least we were in Lübeck!

Charlie Metz:

I do not know when the official close-out date for Lübeck was. All I know is that on or about 18 May, 1965, I led a convoy of 21 vehicles from Lübeck to Rothwesten during the process of close-out. That left twelve trucks, one sedan, and a 25-passenger bus plus the personnel still remaining in Lübeck. It took a long time to close down the site, billets, and the houses. All post, camp, and station property belonging to Bremerhaven had to be returned, i.e. mess hall equipment, beds, and other furniture and appliances on hand receipt from Bremerhaven. Also, I don't know what was required to clear the site to satisfy the German government - like whether they required the security fence to be removed or what was done with the PSP vehicle matting in the vehicle park at the motor pool. Other things that might have affected the close-out date included the condition of the billets. If the walls were smudged or paint chipped, you could be required to paint the place. It was very difficult turning anything back to the German government - it must be in like-new and ready-for-occupancy condition before they will accept it back. The last I remembered about Lübeck was when the antenna installation team hauled the antenna towers back to Rothwesten, either in June or July. Shortly after that I was transferred to Wobeck, so as to the official close-out of Lübeck, I cannot say.

Word has it that the final days of Lübeck were one wild party, with much merriment mixed with the sad duty of tearing down and packing the huts, secret equipment, explosive charges, the antenna, and anything else worth keeping. One day was spent attempting the novelty of cow riding, which I'm sure was a big hit with the cows. And the farmer. However, in true Lübecker fashion, the closing was commemorated with a coat and tie dinner in one of Lübeck finest dining establishments. Prosit!

On December 31, 1976, the United States Army Security Agency as a special entity ceased to exist.

Thus Sprach **Ernie Serna:**
After only four months in Rothwesten, my duffel bag and I were thrown into the back of a deuce-and-a-half - destination Lübeck. As a young PFC I had no knowledge of the city, its exact location, its people or its rich history. As a young kid who had never been outside of Texas, I thought I was being banished to some hell-hole at the end of the world

So it was just by a stroke of luck that I ended up in one of the most beautiful, quaint, historic and romantic cities I have ever seen, then or now. To top it off, a city so full of the most beautiful women I have ever seen anywhere in my travels, even to this day. It is for these reasons that I keep going back every two or three years to visit friends and relive some of those wild and wonderful memories of those years.

I left there two and a half years later, but not alone, and with a lot of lasting memories.

Well said, Ernie, well said. Lübeck was a personal Camelot for a lot of us and it was truly *A Wonderful Moment in Time.*

102. Site overgrown with weeds, 2001

103. Deserted site taken from motorglider in 2000 by D. Wrench

Post Script: Life after Lübeck
CHAPTER 33: Later Contacts

The Lübeck experience is not over. The times change and the bones begin to creak, but the memories still linger. Since I started writing this, I have been in touch with dozens of former Lübeckers through the internet and through personal communing at reunions. Jim Miller, Jim Shaw, Jack Weber, and Mort Weston have been especially helpful in jogging my memory - and getting some facts straight. Universally they say that Lübeck was best summed up by Dave Black's, *"I've learned that I found Camelot when I was 19 years old, and have been trying to regain it ever since."*

Dave can't believe that he was that poetic, but that's his actual quote.

Since my revelatory dream described at the beginning of this chronicle got me re-interested in finding my "roots" in Lübeck, some really, really, strange things have happened. One of the strangest and least plausible and, frankly, beyond belief, deals with my attempts to find the enigmatic Carole again.

I almost became obsessed with finding her again. Not because I wanted to make personal contact again to renew an old romance, but because that's the way I am. I wanted to get her permission to include her letters; although it really wasn't necessary, I thought it would be the right thing to do. Once I started on this quest, that turned out to be far more difficult than I could ever have imagined, I had to, just had to, see the challenge through to completion.

One of my limitations was that I could spend little or no money in this search; that meant hiring a private detective was out, and so was making a personal journey down to Georgia and searching through old newspapers and county records. The internet was my only hope.

To avoid promoting any one web site, I'll just say that I used various genealogical sites and searched through most of them. This was truly difficult, since I had no knowledge of her parents or any other members of her family. I was shooting blanks. I didn't even know if she was still alive or maybe living in France.

Perhaps she didn't want to be found.

This all changed with my son's wedding. He finally met the girl of his dreams at a conference in Tampa Bay. He came home all excited and said I met this chick that is truly awesome and I really like her. After a long distance courtship, from Madison to Tampa Bay, they finally decided to end it all and get married. She moved up north and they planned their big day which turned out pretty much as planned; they were married.

One of the bridesmaids came all the way from Florida where she had been working with the happy bride. Her name was Barbara Townsend and she was originally from Georgia. Before she left for home, I asked her if she would ask around her friends and acquaintances to see if they may have heard of this Carole person. She said she would and I thought, "Yah, all right. That's the last I'll hear of that." I fully expected this was just another thing, like "let's get together sometime" and sometime never comes.

However shortly after, I got the following e-mail from Barb:
About Carole.................you won't believe it! When talking to my Mom on the phone, I asked her to ask my Dad if he knew Carole. From the background, I heard Dad say, " I do. Her father was in the cotton business".........I couldn't believe it! He went out on a blind date with her, but not sure if they dated again. He was even able to dig up a picture of them attending a party. He told me that her family was quite wealthy... and he believes she lives somewhere around Atlanta, now. Can you believe it????

A miracle! Out of approximately 300 million people in this country, Barb asks just **one** and he turns out to know the elusive, formerly young, damsel. Barb went on to say she would send me a copy of the old photo of her dad and Carole. Apparently, they dated only once but it must have been a doozy!

Barb wrote about the photograph: *"It was taken at the Old South Ball, Kappa Alpha Fraternity dance, March 1951, Biltmore Hotel. K A brothers from University of Georgia, Emory University attended. The bands were Tommy & Jimmy Dorsey. (WOW!) The picture was taken at the Piedmont Driving Club. Carole & my Dad were a blind date, and to my knowledge, did not really date her after that."*

104. Carole

Seemed strange to be going to such a high-falutin' ball on a blind date, but they must have done things differently down there. This amazing revelation rekindled my manhunt and knowing that Carole lived somewhere around the huge capital of Georgia made my search a little easier. Finally, I found a name and phone number that seemed to match her relatively well. In fact I was sure it was her. But now that I had it, I couldn't force myself to make the call. I didn't know if it was the right thing to do or if I would even be welcome plus I was just plain scared.

I sat on it for several weeks; then one night, I just said to hell with it, ignored my knocking knees, picked up the phone and dialed the number. A gentleman answered. *Hallooo.*

Hello, my name is Don Johnson and I'm calling to see if a former Carole Boucher lives there.

Yes, indeed. This is her husband. We've been expecting your call. Would you like to speak to her?

Of course, what do you expect after I've been looking for her for months, was what I would have said if I wasn't so polite, but I merely said, "that would be nice." So, they were expecting my call. Apparently some of my earlier probes had hit home.

Carole got on the phone and still had the same soft southern belle voice that I remembered and we chatted for maybe 20 minutes and exchanged e-mail addresses and caught up a bit after 40 some odd years of separation.

A few days later I e-mailed her a brief summary of my life since those golden olden days and told her I would send her some photos and a couple chapters of the book. I told her about Barb's dad and the amazing odds of finding someone that actually knew her and asked if she could remember anything about our times together or maybe had some photographs that I could borrow.

She replied:

Astonishing!! My brother- in-law just finished his memoirs and he would apprise me from time to time of the people he had uncovered during his long search of facts and people. You writers have great resolve and a penchant for detail which I admire. I'm truly amazed .... As I explained, I did not keep a diary during my stay in Paris. You have remembered more of that particular time in Capri and Paris than I. I'm afraid I cannot add much to help you.

I will say that my year in France was a life changing experience, as one might expect. You have had the great fortune of living in several different countries and you know what I mean. One doesn't come away and return to business as usual. I'm a staunch defender of the French and the Parisians in particular. They do not present themselves before the rest of the world as a warm and fuzzy people and, indeed, they are not. Once I realized that all they really want in life is to get their emperor back, life became a little easier. Soft, Southern ways are the antithesis of what they are all about.

Once I learned to play the game I knew I had arrived. By that time it was time to come home. If you are at all interested in knowing everything there is to know about the French, you should read a book titled "Paris to the Moon". The author has them nailed. It's a good read and I recommend it. We have also done some traveling through the years but in our quest to go to different places, we always put off going to Paris. When I did return just three years ago, it was not quite like I left it (they had the audacity to go and wash the buildings) but close enough to have a real trip of nostalgia. How does the song go - the time has come and gone but the memory lingers on. And I hope it always will. Good luck, Don in the writing of your book. I'm sorry I have not been able to contribute much. I could write volumes about life in general as I perceived it but then that would be my book and not yours. I look forward to seeing a copy on the library shelf one of these days . Best wishes to you and your family. Carole

I sent off a package of photos of Paris and a few chapters of the book and apparently something scared her for shortly thereafter, I received the following e-mail:

Don - I appreciate so much the package containing the excerpts from your book and the absolutely lovely photographs of Paris. Seems you have dual talents and if I were you I'd give up my day job. I enjoyed reading parts of your book. For what it's worth, I find your narrative to be strong and imaginative, making for a very good read. You're sure to do well with it. I must tell you, however, that my strong sense of privacy prevails and upon reflection I must ask that you not use my last name in your book (maiden or married). In all honesty, a small part of me is greatly flattered by the attention but the greater part feels strangely unsettled by all this. Call it a southernism or just simply a quirk of an older lady. I am sure you will honor my request. May the rest of the chapters come easily for you. Good luck with the book and the ones to come. The best of health and happiness to you in 2002 and the years beyond. Carole

I wrote back:

Dear former Carole Boucher, from Athens, GA; that's why I sent the excerpts. I did not want and do not want to do anything that will make you feel uncomfortable. I suspect hearing from me after 43 years has been uncomfortable enough. A lot of the book comes from my imagination and a little logical thinking, since I can't remember everything; it's just based on fact, like most movies. Readers can decide for themselves what they want to believe or not. And probably not more than a 100 people (all Lübecker guys) will ever read it, anyway. If that. (I always thought it would be easier to sell 10 books for $70,000 each than 70,000 books for $10.00 each.)

I hope your new name is OK. Please feel flattered, and not unsettled; no one, including you, will even know it may have been you.

Over and out; please let me know if this name is OK and then I will recede into the distant background for another 44 years. dj

Dear DJ, Thanks for humoring the old girl. In my next life I plan on being a better sport. The name works. You have my permission to make her utterly fascinating. And so it goes...
Carole

Message received. OK and thanks for being a part of my life, long ago. dj

However, I had to break my word.

Good morning, Carole; I apologize for the intrusion, especially since I said I would fade into the background, but I seriously would appreciate whatever help you can offer. I'm at the point in my chronicle where I'm interweaving your letters with events or vice versa. (This is really difficult!) Needless to say, your letters are often more interesting than the events. In re-reading your letters and trying to construct a time line and get things a bit more straight in my head, I found that I was confused about some dates and just outright forgot about others. (I think my brain cells have welded some events together.) AND I would like to get things as accurate as can be expected after all these

201

years. Here's what I have reconstructed: Met on Capri around April 15; Met again in Paris for a day or two a few days later. (I have really been detectivating on this since much of my info comes from looking at old slides of Paris/Capri/etc and dating them according to which batch of slides they're in. A sample is attached: Eiffel Tower in mid April, 1958.) Were supposed to meet again to tour the World's Fair on my birthday, which was May 24. I don't remember a single thing about that supposed meeting. Not a single thing. You wrote me two days earlier that you would see me in two days, but there's not one mention of the trip in follow up letters, which seems strange. Apparently, we met at The Fair, then came back to Paris where we got involved in the mob following De Gaulle's coming takeover, which, I found, after extensive internet research, happened on June 1. (Apparently the demonstration was on May 31st or thereabouts.) I have some color slides from the same roll that were taken partly at The Fair and partly in Paris - some of them from the top of the Eiffel Tower.

Any clarification on The Fair and subsequent visit to Paris would be greatly appreciated. Apparently you were in Brussels as in the last letter I have, copied way below, you make reference to the American pavilion. I also realize that time fuzzes memory & wonder if Dickie is still around, could she provide some insight? I now have copied your letters into the manuscript where they can be moved around as needed and include portions of some of them to hopefully jog your memories a bit. (Underhanded of me, of course.) (But I'm desperate.)

ALSO, as I sludge my way through this, incorporating your letters and other letters/notes/etc. I think it would be fitting to have a prologue, written by some of the people involved. Hopefully, by you, as well, that would sort of sum up their memories of that era & give a brief description of what they've been up to all these years. Could be fun. I hope to have this all finished by the end of the summer. I leave for Italy on Saturday for a nine day tour, then will be in Ireland for a week or two in June. So, time's awastin'.

My best to you and your family,
dj
And then I included some of her letters.

105. Brussels – U.S. Pavilion, 1958

She answered:

I've been faking a good mind and body for the last several years, but I think I've been caught. I cannot possibly remember those dates as I did not keep a diary and my slides became mildewed along the way and can not be seen too well by the human eye. I do remember our meeting in Paris in the Eiffel Tower environs and I do remember the "demonstrations" in the city that night. I, like you, do not remember another meeting in Paris. If I were you, I think I would go with what you have. I will never challenge you on this. Sorry I can't conjure up more but there it is. By the way, I think you've doctored those letters a bit, which is fine with me. I could never lay claim to penning such compelling thoughts and observances. Anytime anyone makes me look good, I'm grateful. Have a great trip to Italy and once again I apologize for the failing brain cells. CB

Carole, don't underestimate yourself. The letters are ALL yours, every word, except for maybe one or two that were misspelled. One last question & then I'll fake it from there. Did you or did you not go to the Worlds' Fair in Brussels??? Thanks for your time & I plan on contacting you once more, when the book is finished, so I can send you a copy. Fair enough? dj

We did go to the World's Fair but our time was cut in half because we had driven there in a Deux Chevaux - 2 horse power car with manual windshield wipers and a lawn mower engine. We had lots of car trouble and spent most of our time in Flemish- speaking car repair garages. We did have a whole day at the Fair and I thought it was truly wonderful and still do. This is where I thought we first met up with you and your pal. The sequence of events has certainly become muddled in my mind and that's why I'm really lousy help to you. Sooooo - take it away - over and out.
CB

Thanks, I'm relieved. You confirm my foggy remembrances; I vaguely remember being with you & Dickie & that gray junkpile with a cloth top in a muddy field or parking lot near some farmer's house who was renting out rooms right on the edge of the fair. I don't recall much about wandering around the grounds, like did we actually meet under the Atomium, but I definitely remember many of the individual exhibitions and pavilions. (I think that's what got me to go into design.) Apparently, from there, we went to Paris and got caught in the De Gaulle demonstration. The decision to return to Paris is the part that bugs me. At least that's how I'll write it. Thanks, again and I won't ask you to make a trip to your friendly neighborhood regressive hypnotist. (Although I may try it myself.) I've got the sequence right now, and just have to fill in the details.

Have a nice spring! dj

CHAPTER 34: Strange How Things Happen

One day I received the following e-mail:

Hi Don...

Are you the same Don Johnson that I went to London with on leave...way back when? I'm Richard Strader and I think I met you in Bremerhaven..not sure though. Before Lübeck..I was stationed in Bremerhaven and before that in Wesendorf..not too far from the guys in Bardorf and Helmstedt. I haven't been able to contribute too much to the Lübeck Assn because of time constraints related to my work. However I have tons of pictures and memories of my time in Germany ..and of course..the Lübeck experience. ...

I found and communicate infrequently with Jim Long (JG) and Irv (BMF) Deranger who were part of my DF crew while in Lubeck.

I've written all this assuming that you are the one I went to London with, but the photo of the young stud-muffin looks exactly like the guy that went to London with me. Let me know If I'm on target..or owe some look-alike an apology.

Dick Strader

We e-mailed back and forth for some weeks which led to the discovery that, indeed, Dick and I had gone to London together and he knew the mysterious stranger that I couldn't remember, the one I had gone to Capri with, as Irv Deranger, who was in his DF unit. He also e- mailed some of his photographs.

...If you don't recognize me then I'm the wrong person. If memory serves I went to London with a chap by the name of Don Johnson..who looks a hell of a lot like you in that group pic you sent from Lübeck. We stayed in a B&B operated by a lady who only would admit people who presented her with her card which she would give to any one who stayed in her place and didn't tear it up or bring girls back for an orgy. I have many Black & White photos in my scrapbook of that trip which I will have to scan. Since time is of the essence,.I can't promise just when I'll get to it.

*The small thumbnail pic you sent looks for all the world like
Irv Deranger. As you probably know..his wife is now on line
according to Miller who recently posted a "Found Lübecker" to
the group.*

*Again..my apologies for being so tardy in responding..
Cheers...
Dick Strader*

Dick; Thanks for your instantaneous reply. With respects to
remembering Dick Strader: I was forming an image in my mind
of a tallish curly haired guy but couldn't put a face on it. I
remember Kehrli, who was from Iowa and died a few years ago.
Now that you mention it, I remember the B&B and I think we
stayed upstairs in some tiny room. (Low-ceilinged and stairs that
went to the left at the top.) (Purple? carpet or linoleum pops up
through my now connecting synapses.)

I appreciate your thoughtfulness & time. dj

Don;

*I just finished scanning some of the photos and mementos
from my scrapbook. (born journalist...I saved everything) I have
included a set of orders...some theater tickets...and the boat
ticket...and some pages of photos that I did not scan individually.
However is there are any in the pages...numbers 1-5...let me
know what page...which pic..and I'll rescan individually.*

*I could not find the pic of you in my B&W stuff...but then not
all went in the scrap book. The B&W stuff pales in to
comparison to the color slides I have. ...*

*I always loved photography..but I don't hold a candle to your
expertise from the shots I've seen on your web page..but I gave it
a good go. I had to give it up as a hobby because it became
frightfully expensive and then too..I got busy with many other
things. I now have a digital camera and a web cam and ScanJet
4200C.*

*I've also started my memoirs..not that I'm a famous person
or ever intend for it to be published..but it is for my children who
really only know me as their Father. Not who/what/when/where
before their awareness nor after they grew up and moved away. I
had to belay that project though...because of lack of time. ...*

*BTW...did you recognize the photo of me with Kehrli? Scott
Messinger..Irv Deranger..J.G. Long.. Fitchett..Graham.. J.P.
Ford and others were in my DF team. I'm only going to add a
few attachments at a time so as to not crash your pooter.*
    Later.......
    Dick Strader

Dick;

    Thanks for the photos; I'm looking forward to receiving
more. I recognize a lot of the troopers. Kerhli, Al McCrumb,
now in Nebraska, Bill McMaster, with the horn, Wes Roche,
now in Minnesota, I think, Chick Rogers, Lt. Bell, who was at
the last reunion, retired as a Colonel, I think, Jim Bruce, who
died a couple years ago, Also a profile of Duain Shaw in front of
the 2 movie projectors.

    Can't recall the name of the "stout" guy leaning on the rock
at the Grenze crossing, (maybe Scott Messenger) or the guy
singing into the broom or the one playing the guitar. They look
familiar, though. A guy sitting on the bed (3/4 face) looks like
Deranger. One of the guys playing cards, light sweater, v neck,
looks like me, but I can't be sure. The back of the head in that
same picture looks like it belonged to Wes Roche.

    FLASH! I just discovered indisputable proof that we were
there together. Look at your photo of Trafalgar Square, with the
statue on the left and the lion sort of in the far right center and
another "column base" on the right. Well, one of the pictures I
sent to you is of the identical scene. The family sitting on a
bench in the lower left is the same. It looks as though you took
your pic a few seconds after I took mine. dj

    How about that? Lübeckers forever!

106. (above) My shot of Trafalgar Square

107. Dick's shot a few second later; look at lower left corner

108. Dick Strader & Marcus Kehrli on dock behind J-House

109. Border marker; why we were there. Never forget!
Photo by Duain Shaw

110 and 111. JW House renovated and painted yellow and white; 2001

112. Riverboat, 2001

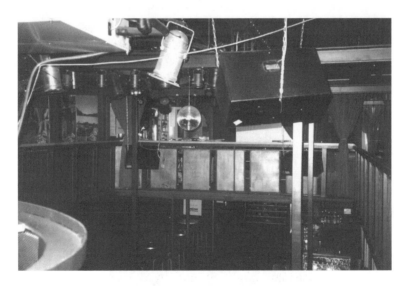

113. New Riverboat interior

114. Harbor view, 2001

115. *Kohlmarkt und Marienkirche, 2001*

116. Eventide, Lübeck

CHAPTER 35: THE FINAL CHAPTER

117. Hubert

Totally Unrelated To Us Lübeckers - But Then Again, Maybe It Isn't

We had a cat named Hubert. He was a beautiful fluffy, long-haired orange-colored Persian-type barn cat. His mother had distemper, so when Hubert was born, he couldn't walk, talk, or handle his basic needs. Like eating. My daughter, Anne, rescued Hubert and took him under her wing and helped him learn how to walk and take care of himself. As a result of his mother's conditions, Hubert's back end and front end weren't too coordinated, but he managed to prosper and grow.

He grew into a beautiful strong cat and soon became the "boss" of our small herd of cats and the family baby. He didn't know he was handicapped, but he would always walk sort of funny, with his tail dragging like a fluffy orange crocodile. And he could seldom run in a straight line, as his butt end kept trying to outpace his head.

When called for supper, which was held in the basement where they were kept for the night, he would often come barreling through the dining room, do a couple loopy-loops, like a car on slick ice, bounce off a wall, circle through the kitchen and finally down the stairs through the kitty door to his food.

There was always a "whomp" as he went through the door since he banged it fiercely. Luckily, I think his condition dulled his pain receptors because he seldom showed any signs of pain.

When Hubert wanted to sit on your lap, he would pause for a moment, maybe as long as 10 or 15 seconds, gather up the various un-coordinated parts of his body, and leap. Sometimes, he would fly right on by, landing against the wall, or somewhere up near your face. Other times, he would misjudge only to come floating straight down to a feathery lap-landing. Then he would sit there and preen himself with pride.

One day we came home and Hubert had jumped clear up to the dining room table, where he was comfortably asleep. He was generally peaceful, but could become fierce when riled by one of the other cats and they learned not to instigate things. On one trip to the vet to clean his anal glands, never a pleasing prospect for all those concerned, it took four people to hold him down.

One day, we noticed that Hubert looked uncomfortably fat, even like he was bloating, so it meant another trip to the vet, whom he despised, due to his earlier experience with his glands. I guess he had finally learned what pain was - and he didn't like it. Hubert was diagnosed with cancer. But this kind in cats was usually treatable with pills and chemo-therapy.

For the first weeks, this meant a trip to the vet twice a week. The office was 10 miles away, with Hubert bitching and moaning the whole way. On top of it all, he hated to take pills and the chemo meant sticking a needle into a vein in the front leg, which was totally painful and obviously distressing to the poor cat.

After about six weeks, Hubert was cured.

Or so we thought.

Several months later, he began to bloat again, so back to the vet we went. He had suffered a relapse and the cancer was back. After one trip, with Hubert fighting and yowling the whole time as he was jabbed in the front leg with the life-extending needle, we decided the cure was worse than the disease. With the vet's agreement, we decided to let nature take its course. He would either be OK or not, but he wouldn't have to suffer the excruciating pain of the treatment and the horrible thoughts he had on the way to the vets.

Things went along well for a couple months, but we could tell that he was still slowly bloating. But Hubert didn't realize he was sick. He ate, drank, fought, and kept on with his life like he always had. We were amazed at how he handled all this; if you didn't know, you wouldn't realize he had a terminal condition.

One night, I herded the cats downstairs to be fed, and I remember Hubert chowing down with his usual gluttony - he never missed a meal - and he sat there after eating, licking his paws in contentment.

The next morning, I went down to give the cats their breakfast and let them upstairs for the day. I doled out their tidbits, but Hubert wasn't there. I called, "Hubert. Hubert - breakfast time," figuring he was up on the storage shelves somewhere and couldn't get down or maybe laying sick somewhere.

I searched for a bit and found him lying under a chair, curled up slightly in a ball. He was dead. (Tears are welling up in my eyes right now and this was over four years ago.) His body was still warm so I picked him up and carried him upstairs and just lost it. Lost it completely. I cursed myself for not going down earlier as maybe he would have still been alive and somehow saved. I sobbed and moaned unlike any other time in my life. Our baby Hubert was gone. Gone forever.

I took him for one last trip to the vet, so he could be autopsied, since they were curious as to what was slowly killing him. They found he died because the fluid from cancer of the liver had accumulated around his heart and it just shut down. He died peacefully, without pain, in his sleep.

I left him to be cremated. When I got home from the vet, I went back to the basement, because I had noticed some fluid leaking from Hubert's mouth and I wanted to clean it up. When I moved the chair under which he had taken his last sleep, I saw this image, almost like a drawing or intaglio print of Hubert's body. The hairs on my neck stood straight up. I couldn't believe it and I started crying all over again. "Hubert, you've left something for us to see, but I'll be damned if I know what it means."

Close examination of the image (Shroud of St. Hubert?) revealed what looked like his two ears and fluffy mane and tail and legs and then I looked even closer and saw the profile of his face. Even an eye. I speculate that when he died, he sort of went uhhhh - ohhhhh in a typical spastic Hubert moment and left two images of his head at the instant of his passing.

Of course, I showed the image to my wife and kids and anyone who came over and they found it to be as unbelievable as I did. I took multiple photos to be sure it was recorded and, frankly, didn't know if I should call the Pope or the National Enquirer. My vet said he had never seen anything like it and I even showed the pictures to a radiology friend at the university and he was as puzzled as anyone. It had to be some chemical reaction to the concrete, but what?

The image is still there and I will allow no one to touch it, although it does come up with water. I had to build a protective dike around it last fall when the septic system got tree-rooted and backed up a bit. Luckily just a little bit.

What does it all mean? I have no logical explanation. But, as all of us old-time Lübeckers are aging, I look at it as some message from Hubert that said,

"Thanks for your kindness and your care. And especially your love. I'll see ya later."

So maybe this tale of "St. Hubert" has some meaning for us Lübeckers after all and in closing, may I be so honored as to repeat, "I'll see ya later."

118. St. Hubert, positive image

119. St. Hubert, negative image